the fundamentals of
interior architecture
john coles & naomi house

An AVA Book
Published by AVA Publishing SA
Rue des Fontenailles 16
Case Postale
1000 Lausanne 6
Switzerland
Tel: +41 786 005 109
Email: enquiries@avabooks.ch

Distributed by Thames & Hudson (ex-North America)
181a High Holborn
London WC1V 7QX
United Kingdom
Tel: +44 20 7845 5000
Fax: +44 20 7845 5055
Email: sales@thameshudson.co.uk
www.thamesandhudson.com

Distributed in the USA and Canada by:
Watson-Guptill Publications
770 Broadway
New York, NY 10003
Fax: +1 646 654 5487
Email: info@watsonguptill.com
www.watsonguptill.com

English Language Support Office
AVA Publishing (UK) Ltd.
Tel: +44 1903 204 455
Email: enquiries@avabooks.co.uk

ISBN 2-940373-38-8 and 978-2-940373-38-3

10 9 8 7 6 5 4 3 2 1

Design by Gavin Ambrose
www.gavinambrose.co.uk

Production by
AVA Book Production Pte. Ltd., Singapore
Tel: +65 6334 8173
Fax: +65 6259 9830
Email: production@avabooks.com.sg

Cover image © photobank.ch

the fundamentals of

interior architecture

john coles & naomi house

contents

0 1 2

Introduction

SPACE/form

SITE/function

How to get the most
out of this book   6

Introduction   8

Space & place   16
Elements & composition
of interior space   24

Analysing the site   46
Types of interior   58

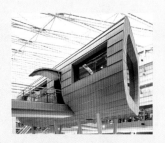

3 4 5 6

3 MATERIALS/texture

Understanding
the interior   78
Selecting materials   88
Perception of quality   98
Architectural materials 108

4 LIGHT/mood

Understanding light   120
Using light   130
Calculating light   142

5 PRESENTATION/representation

Key stages in design 148
Representing design   154

6 Conclusion

Conclusion   170
Sources of information
   and inspiration   172
Buildings of interest   173
Index   174
Acknowledgements
   and credits   176

how to get the most out of this book

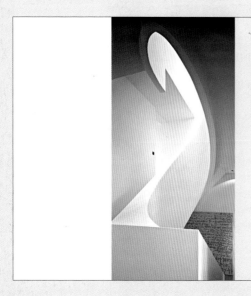

There is no limit to the type or size of building that can fall within the practice of the interior architect and, equally, no limit to the range of activities which they may design. This chapter will explore the way in which the existing building affects the designer's response to the client's brief and will identify the devices used by the designer in order to achieve the appropriate spatial and functional experience.

1

Chapters
Each chapter opens with an introductory spread containing a brief precis and image.

Navigation
Chapter titles are shown in the top-left of every spread, page numbers in the right. Sub-section titles are also shown at the bottom-right of each spread.

Section openers
Each sub-section opens with a list of topics to be covered and a brief introductory text.

---

elements & composition of interior space

in this section

plane / scale / proportion / vista / movement / transition / accessibility

The following section introduces the elements, and the vocabulary used to describe them, that are key to the creation and understanding of interior architecture. These elements can be used to express the character and quality of the interior, and used either individually or as a combination, will impart atmosphere and personality.

plane
The plane is the most fundamental element of interior architecture. Essentially a two-dimensional form, it serves, when employed as floors, walls and ceilings, to enclose and define space. Smaller planar elements contribute doors, stairs and other interior elements such as shelves and furniture. As well as enclosing and modulating space, the plane becomes the carrier of the required material, texture and colour qualities of the interior as well as, by absorption or reflection, controlling acoustic and lighting values.

The absence of a plane, or the perforation of one, may be used to direct attention to some other part of the site or interior as well as permitting physical movement and the passage of light, air and sound.

The realities of construction mean that built planes have thickness. How much of that thickness is visible (or, indeed, whether it is accentuated for aesthetic purposes) is a judgement for the designer to make. In traditional architecture the massive materials employed ensure that, where visible, the edge of the plane will have substantial thickness; but the advent of new materials and processes permits slimmer structures and this slimness is often used as an expression of modernity. A building providing excellent illustration of the expressive use of planar structures is Schröder House. Designed by Gerrit Rietveld it reads, both inside and out, as a series of independent slim planar elements virtually hovering in space.

Thomas Cook, Accoladia, view of restaurant at office fit-out (left)
Location London, UK
Date 2002
Designer Bluebottle
This seating environment for Thomas Cook Holidays uses plane elements to define space, separating one activity from another, while the partitions give clues as to what lies behind the plane.
Photograph courtesy of Paris Burrows

Chapter 1 / SPACE/form

elements & composition of interior space

the fundamentals of interior architecture
SPACE/form

36/37

Le Corbusier claimed that 'a stair separates – a ramp connects', and it is certainly true that the ramp contains possibilities of flow and gentle transition that the fundamentally jerky movement (both visually and practically) of the staircase finds difficult to embody. Like all architectural devices the ramp has both pragmatic and aesthetic qualities that have been employed in different proportions for different reasons throughout history. The important point about ramps is that to be effortless in use they need to be shallow, but being shallow means that they need to be lengthy and it is often difficult in real-world situations to accommodate that length. In the case of Richard Meier, who has used ramps more consistently than any other contemporary architect, a significant proportion of the building volume is devoted to ramp access (look at the Museum of Contemporary Art in Barcelona and the Museum of Decorative Arts in Frankfurt). Many years earlier Frank Lloyd Wright had adopted a different approach when creating the Guggenheim Museum in New York by winding the ramp into a spiral

around a hollow, cone-shaped void. In doing so he created a system that was both gallery space and access system and which, while presenting problems to exhibition curators ever since, created an iconic building.

Escalators and lifts work slightly differently. Glass lifts, particularly those climbing the external façade, are no longer a novelty but still have a powerful appeal. In many ways the escalator provides a composite of the experience of lift, ramp and stair because of its self-propelled trajectory; but so often the form and materials of the device itself and the awkward transition between human and mechanical propulsion at the beginning and end of the journey are less than satisfactory. However, here too glass is playing an increasing role in diminishing the slab-sided aspect of the traditional installation so that one hopes that in the not-too-distant future the sculptural form will achieve the refinement that it deserves.

'I strive for an architecture from which
nothing can be taken away.'
Helmut Jahn

Frank Lloyd Wright (USA)
1867–1959
Notable projects:
Fallingwater, Pennsylvania, USA
Guggenheim Museum, New York, USA
Prairie House, New York, USA
A key figure in interiors, Lloyd Wright is frequently credited with instigating the move away from single-function, box-like room living to a more communal, shared space concept. Using simple

materials, he experimented with screening devices, subtle changes in ceiling height and floating planar elements in order to do this. Wright practised what is known as organic architecture, making use of simple materials such as brick, wood and plaster. During his lifetime he was also instrumental in the move to begin protecting old buildings. The Frank Lloyd Wright Foundation now exists to conserve the work of the architect and advance the organic method of architecture and teaching that he promoted.

London Loft, staircase view (left)
Location: London, UK
Date: 2004
Designer: Jonathan Stickland
This staircase is not simply a functional device – it provides a strong sculptural focal point to the space
Photograph by James Morris <www.jamesmorris.info>, provided courtesy of Jonathan Stickland

Image captions
Each image is displayed with an accompanyig caption, giving details of the project depicted as well as the specific view shown.

Quotations
Quotations from well-known interior architects and designers are used to put content into context.

Architect biographies
Throughout the book, the reader can find out about the work of practising architects and designers who have contributed to the subject of interior architecture.

the fundamentals of interior architecture
questions in summary

116/117

questions in summary
architectural materials

1 2 3 4 5 6 7 8

| What range of materials and finishes are available to the interior architect? | To what elements does timber lend itself well? | What sort of environment does stone and marble create? | How can the interior architect make use of concrete and terrazzo? | What sort of responses can metallic materials invoke? | For what elements might glass be suitable? | What range of plastics is available to the interior architect? | How can the choice of fabric create coloured, textures and patterned effects? |

Questions in summary
Each sub-section ends with a selection of questions, designed to summarise what has just been discussed.

how to get the most out of this book

Open the door of any building, in any part of the world, and enter. As you do so you will be aware that, with no conscious effort on your part, you experience a response to the space beyond the door. Subsequent responses may reinforce or modify that first one. These sensations are not accidental. They are the result of the senses (sight, sound, smell and touch) conveying messages to the brain, which analyses them with reference to previous experience, to a sense of balance and proportion and to a psychological (and often very personal) reaction to the stimuli of light, colour and acoustics.

It is these sensations that the effective designer orchestrates in the design of interiors and which we experience when we enter them. Of course there is more to this than generating a theatrical experience. Using the skills and understanding borne of study and practice, the designer is endeavouring to create an environment that not only feels appropriate, but also functions in a way that supports the needs of its users.

The term 'interior architecture' emerged in the 1970s as the description of a discipline that employs architectural theory, history and principles in the design and creation of interior space. Its growth was in part due to a perception that by employing the rigour of architectural thinking together with the sensory understanding of interior design, a synthesis could be produced that was both intellectually and humanistically satisfying, and which overcame the narrow specialisms of façade-driven architecture and context-free interior design that were prevalent at that time.

At a more pragmatic level, the use of the term 'interior architecture' is a response to the uncertainties inherent in the title 'interior design'. These uncertainties have been accentuated by the increasing use, in magazine articles and television makeover programmes, to describe the process of choosing curtains, furnishings and surface treatments: activities which might be better titled 'interior decoration'.

Over the course of the last thirty years the title 'interior architecture' has acquired a growing acceptance and an increasing sense of identity. That identity is distinguished by the following ideas:

- It acknowledges and respects the enclosing structure and its context as initiators of design strategies.
- It is an activity that is involved in the manipulation and enjoyment of three-dimensional space.
- It employs the sensory stimuli of sound, touch, smell and sight as essential parts of the interior experience.
- It recognises light as a medium for defining space, creating effect and producing well-being.
- It employs materials and colour as integral components of the designed environment.

Millennium Dome, rest zone (facing page)

Location: London, UK

Date: 2000

Designer: Richard Rogers

Not all designed spaces have a particular function. The form, colour and light quality of this space combine to create a meditative experience with which the user can connect both physically and emotionally.

Photograph courtesy of Jonathan Mortimer

In terms of philosophy and practice interior architecture is a discipline that is heavily (although not exclusively) involved with the remodelling and repurposing of existing buildings and so has an important role to play in the sustainable reuse of the built environment. This reuse finds expression in an enormously wide range of buildings and activities. There is no building, however grand or humble, that is exempt from the interior architect's portfolio. Palaces, hotels, airports, offices, department stores, restaurants, railway stations, corner shops and apartments all offer the opportunity to reformulate, update and improve living and working environments. To undertake this work requires an ability to analyse the existing building and its environs, to understand the needs of the client and the wider society and to generate a concept and a design that creates a synergetic relationship between these elements.

The role of the interior architect will vary from practitioner to practitioner and from commission to commission. It will involve understanding and interpreting the needs of a client, who may be an individual, a public organisation or a commercial business, and creating a collaboration with other professionals: architects, structural engineers, craftsmen, quantity surveyors, heating and ventilation engineers among others, to develop a creative response to those needs and to oversee their translation from a concept to a built reality. During this process the interior architect will be responsible for specifying and documenting the myriad decisions and activities required by the building process and will ensure the fulfilment of legal and regulatory obligations. All these things add up to a demanding professional life; but a life in which one is uniquely able to make a real difference to the conditions and experiences of people in their day-to-day lives.

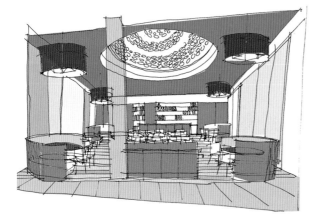

Cuckoo Club, concept sketch (left)

Location: London, UK	
Date: 2005	
Designer: Blacksheep	

A design concept is arrived at once a design brief has been created, and the designer has begun to research the existing building and its context. A design concept is an expression of the key ideas with which the designer intends to work in order to generate a scheme. The image on the left would have been presented to the client in order to communicate the design intentions, and begins to express decisions that have been made about the relationship between form and materials.
Photograph courtesy of Blacksheep

Canary Wharf Underground station (left)

Location: London, UK

Date: 2000

Designer: Foster + Partners

Interior spaces are not always domestic in scale. The cathedral-like quality of Canary Wharf Underground Station celebrates the movement from the subterranean environment of the station platform to the light at ground level.

Photograph courtesy of Jonathan Mortimer

MBAM (Marble Bar Asset Management) trade floor, reception (facing page)

Location: London, UK

Date: 2004

Designer: Blacksheep

Designers continually explore the relationship between the overall design statement that they are making, and the detailed design of individual components of a scheme. The image shown here describes a clean, minimal approach to space and form with no superfluous detail – an approach that is evident both in the formal relationship between key elements and in the treatment of the materials themselves. Note the junction between floor finish and glazed room, and also between the reception desk and its glass top.

Photograph by Francesca Yorke, provided courtesy of Blacksheep

Each chapter in this book introduces and examines the key ideas and processes involved in the practice of interior architecture; describing not only the practical goals and activities but the values and meanings that are incorporated within, and conveyed by, design decisions.

As well as skills and understanding the book introduces the descriptive and technical vocabulary used by the professional designer.

Throughout the book we use the term interior architect as the generic description for someone who practices interior architecture; but it is important to say that not all interior architecture is produced by interior architects. Indeed there are parts of the world, and the United Kingdom is one, where, because of legal limitations on the word architect, there can be no such professional title. Historically, what we would today recognise as interior architecture has been produced by enlightened architects and designers who worked to the principles of the discipline long before they were formally defined, and this continues to be the case today.

'I see architecture not as Gropius did, as a moral venture, as truth, but as invention, in the same way that poetry or music or painting is invention.'
Michael Graves

There is no limit to the type or size
of building that can fall within the
practice of the interior architect
and, equally, no limit to the range
of activities which they may design.
This chapter will explore the way in
which the existing building affects
the designer's response to the
client's brief and will identify the
devices used by the designer in
order to achieve the appropriate
spatial and functional experience.

space & place

In his writings, Le Corbusier identifies the idea of the *tabula rasa* – the blank slate on which design and experience may be written. In particular he pinpoints the concept of starting from nothing and generating a sense of place. Place refers to a particular point in space – one that has either singular or multiple identities, and is often a space that comprises a particular relationship between architecture and site. In recent times it has become increasingly important for us to identify ourselves with the spaces that we occupy and use, and to understand them both physically and emotionally.

understanding the sense of place

Places are spaces with meaning and that meaning is often constructed through time, so that history is seen to be necessary in the creation of place. That history might be accessible to a wide audience or it might be intimate and individual – Trafalgar Square engenders a sense of place that we can all understand in terms of power, but the sense of place that you experience when you walk down the street where you lived as a child may only be understood by you. A sense of place therefore can be both constructed (as in Trafalgar Square) and personal – and these experiences can often overlap.

Understanding the sense of place engendered in a building and its spatial context is an essential aspect of the design process. Very occasionally an architect may be involved in developing from a blank slate in the Corbusian sense; but the interior architect – never. The interior architect's role is to transform, to repurpose: to breathe new life into spaces and places that have a history and existing character but which, because of social or economic pressure, fashion, or simply change of ownership, require a new existence and identity. In order to achieve this transformation the designer must understand the contribution that history has provided and use this to create a design

Battersea Power Station (right)

Location: London, UK

Date: 2008 (projected)

Designer: Universal Design Studio

The industrial past and present of this prime London location provides the designer with an entirely different set of constraints. The surrounding site is as much an issue to consider in any design proposal, as the language and typology of the building itself. Interior architects need to pay close attention to the location in which a project sits, and research into any given site will yield information and material essential to the creation of a successful final scheme.
Photograph courtesy of Universal Design Studio

proposal that – as well as fulfilling the practical and aesthetic requirements of the design brief – understands, respects and engages in a dialogue with the existing building.

There are excellent reasons for employing old buildings in new situations rather than simply demolishing them and starting afresh. In the first place the materials and energy locked into an existing building comprise a form of financial and environmental value that would be expensive to replace. But, perhaps as important, their use enriches our experience by creating a tangible link between the past, present and future.

Within existing buildings there is always evidence of the forms, materials, craftsmanship and details present at its construction, as well as the additions and alterations that have accrued over time. These create a richness and vibrancy with which the designer can work in the creation of the design scheme. The form and proportions of space, the shape and positioning of windows, the surfaces created by materials and structures all contribute to what is sometimes referred to as the *genius loci* – the spirit of the place. It is the interior architect's responsibility to recognise that spirit and to use the qualities and opportunities that it offers.

space & place

the fundamentals of interior architecture
SPACE/form

building reuse

Employing existing buildings will almost inevitably involve work on the **structure** and **fabric** of that building; to stabilise it, improve it or prepare it for its new purpose. This work may be categorised in one of four ways:

Preservation fixes the building in its found state, making no attempt to repair or improve it but ensuring that, so far as such a thing is possible, it is immune from further decay. This could well be an appropriate response to an important building where it would be historically unacceptable to attempt to return it to its original state but where, without such preservation work, the effects of time and weather would result in its ultimate destruction.

Restoration returns the building to its as-built state using period materials and techniques to create the illusion that it has been untouched by time. It should be said that this is a contentious activity, there being a fine line between restoring a building and creating a pastiche.

Renovation renews and updates the building to make it suitable for contemporary life, perhaps by incorporating a modern bathroom, kitchen or heating system. Renovation work implies that there will be no major change of function or form.

Remodelling (referred to as Adaptive Reuse in America) locates an entirely new **function** within an existing building, which may be substantially modified to accept that interjection. As described above it uses the cultural and material capital intrinsic to the building shell to make connections between the old and the new.

It is in the renovation and remodelling of buildings that the majority of interior architects will operate, but these categories are not mutually exclusive and may be used in conjunction with one another in different parts of the project. As an example, the remodelling of the Great Court at the British Museum undertaken by Foster & Partners involved not only a re-skinning of the Reading Room and the creation of the new roof, but also restoration of the existing internal **façades** to remedy years of neglect and misuse.

structure	fabric	function	façade
The arrangements of the various parts of something and often referred to in architecture as the assembled or constructed parts of a building.	The main 'body' of a building – usually the walls, floor and ceiling.	The practical use or purpose of a design.	The exterior planes on the front of a building.

Carlo Scarpa (Italy)

1906–1978
Notable projects:
Castelvecchio Museum, Verona, Italy
Brion–Vega Cemetery, San Vito d'Altivole, Italy

Carlo Scarpa is well known for his deep understanding of raw materials, architectural technique and the history of Venetian art. He resisted the attempts of other twentieth-century architects to strip building methods down to their most functional and simple.

His work has become an inspiration to many architects/designers wishing to revive craft and luxurious materials in a contemporary fashion. Scarpa taught drawing and interior decoration until the late 1970s and, though most of his work is based in northern Italy, he designed buildings, landscapes and gardens as far afield as the USA, Canada and Saudi Arabia. He took much of his inspiration for a project from the existing building so his work was often a long process of archaeology, analysis and construction.

Barbican Tower Apartment, view of bedroom (above)

Location: London, UK

Date: 2004

Designer: Nick Coombe

The long, flush-mounted wall mirror in this Barbican apartment bedroom reflects the spatial context within which the scheme sits, offering a panoramic view of the city. The urban location of this apartment has been celebrated in its interior, which is bright and hard-edged.

Photograph by James Morris <www.jamesmorris.info>, provided courtesy of Nick Coombe

the fundamentals of interior architecture
SPACE/form

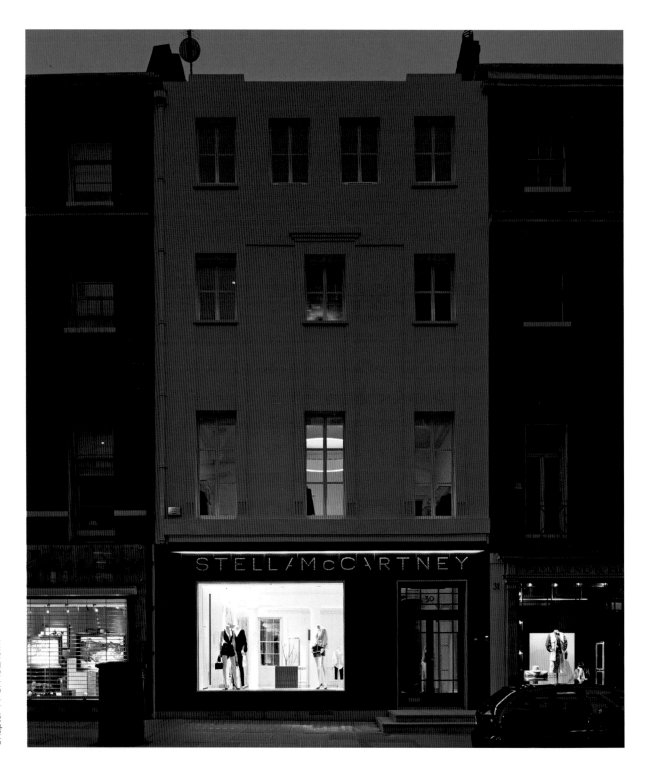

'All over the world, buildings that have been recycled from an earlier function to a new one seem to serve their users better today than they ever did before...'
Peter Blake

Stella McCartney UK flagship store, interior view (right)

Location: London, UK

Date: 2002

Designer: Universal Design Studio

The natural light that floods this interior enters the building through tall openings in the façade. These door/windows were a feature of the building when it was originally constructed, and have been used to their full-effect in this contemporary remodelling – note the lack of screening, which ensures maximum daylight penetration to illuminate the clothing on sale.

Photograph by Richard Davies, provided courtesy of Universal Design Studio

Stella McCartney flagship store, exterior view (facing page)

Location: London, UK

Date: 2002

Designer: Universal Design Studio

Interior architects work with a range of building typologies that establish a number of useful design constraints. The property that houses Stella McCartney's London flagship store perfectly sets the scene for her collection, drawing on its bourgeois history to inform the scheme.

Photograph by Richard Davies, provided courtesy of Universal Design Studio

questions in summary
space & place

1 2

How do we perceive the spaces that we occupy and use?

What makes a space a place?

3 4 5

What is the role
of the interior
architect?

How does the
interior architect
transform and
repurpose a space?

How might the
existing internal
structure influence
the way the interior
architect works with
the interior?

elements & composition of interior space

in this section

plane / scale / proportion / vista / movement / transition / accessibility

The following section introduces the elements, and the vocabulary used to describe them, that are key to the creation and understanding of interior architecture. These elements can be used to express the character and quality of the interior, and used either individually or as a combination, will impart atmosphere and personality.

plane

The plane is the most fundamental element of interior architecture. Essentially a two-dimensional form, it serves, when employed as floors, walls and ceilings, to enclose and define space. Smaller planar elements contribute doors, stairs and other interior elements such as shelves and furniture. As well as enclosing and modulating space, the plane becomes the carrier of the required material, texture and colour qualities of the interior as well as, by absorption or reflection, controlling acoustic and lighting values.

The absence of a plane, or the perforation of one, may be used to direct attention to some other part of the site or interior as well as permitting physical movement and the passage of light, air and sound.

The realities of construction mean that built planes have thickness. How much of that thickness is visible (or, indeed, whether it is accentuated for aesthetic purposes) is a judgement for the designer to make. In traditional architecture the massive materials employed ensure that, where visible, the edge of the plane will have substantial thickness; but the advent of new materials and processes permits slimmer structures and this slimness is often used as an expression of modernity. A building providing excellent illustration of the expressive use of planar structures is Schröder House. Designed by Gerrit Rietveld it reads, both inside and out, as a series of independent slim planar elements virtually hovering in space.

Thomas Cook, Accoladia, view of restaurant at office fit-out (left)

Location: Peterborough, UK

Date: 2001

Designer: Bluebottle

This seating environment for Thomas Cook Holidays uses plane elements to define space, separating one activity from another; the perforations give clues as to what lies behind the plane.

Photograph by Frans Burrows, provided courtesy of Bluebottle

elements & composition of interior space

SPACE/form

scale

The term 'scale' has two meanings for the designer: the first involves a method of drawing buildings to reduce their real-life size to fit the piece of paper we are using. To do this we draw to scale – that is, we visually reduce every part of the design using a chosen ratio. If we are drawing something very large, a plan of the site for instance, we might use a ratio of 1:200 or 1:500, meaning that each thing we draw will be one two-hundredth or one five-hundredth of the size of the real thing. When drawing smaller things, details of cabinetwork perhaps, we may be able to draw things at 1:5 or even full size, while between those extremes, say when drawing the layout of a space, we might employ a scale of 1:50 or 1:100.

The second meaning of scale concerns the apparent size of something in relation to something else. Since the interior architect is usually concerned with providing space for human activity we use the size of a human as that 'something else' and in doing so are able to refer to 'human scale'. If we perceive a space or an object as a comfortable fit with our own dimensions we are able to say that it has human scale.

Patek Philippe, exhibition stand (left)

Location: Basel, Switzerland

Date: 1998

Designer: Virgile and Stone

This glazed elliptical 'pavilion' sits within a large, clear-span space. Rather like a building within a building it retains a form and function independent of the surrounding environment.
Photograph by Ian McKinnel, provided courtesy of Virgile and Stone

Arne Jacobsen (Denmark)

1902–1971

Notable projects:

National Bank of Denmark,

SAS Royal Hotel, Copenhagen

Born in Denmark, Arne Jacobsen made every aspect of an architectural commission his responsibility: the landscape, the building structure and fabric. Even the detail design of door handles and table cutlery were the focus of a rigorous attention to detail, craftsmanship and proportion. As a designer he produced a range of plywood-and-steel (Ant and Series 7) and upholstered (Egg and Swan) furniture, and Cylinda Line tableware. All his work combined modernist ideals of rationalism and simplicity with a Nordic love of naturalism. His integrated approach to design and architecture can be seen in the SAS building in Copenhagen and in St Catherine's College, Oxford. He was educated at the Royal Danish Academy of Fine Arts, School of Architecture and was a professor at the academy from 1956–65.
<www.arne-jacobsen.com>

**Villa Arena Furniture
Shopping Mall (left)**

Location: Amsterdam,
Netherlands

Date: 2001

Designer: Virgile and Stone

The atrium below allows natural
light to filter down into the
circulation areas of this large
shopping complex.

*Photograph by Jannes Linders,
provided courtesy of Virgile and
Stone*

elements & composition of interior space

Eliden, Lotte department store, general view (below)

Location: Seoul, South Korea

Date: 2001

Designer: Universal Design Studio

The proportions of this space emphasise width over height. The patterned glass panels interrupt this horizontally, breaking it down into a number of overlapping components. Note that these elements are the full height of the space.

Photograph courtesy of Universal Design Studio

proportion

Where scale describes the size of elements compared to some standard measure, proportion refers to the dimensional relationship of the design elements – one to another or one to the whole. The human eye recognises the qualities of a space by its proportions in relation to its size. Low-ceilinged spaces of large plan areas will feel oppressive, when a smaller space of the same height might feel entirely comfortable. Very high spaces, as found in cathedrals and important public buildings, can generate a sense of awe and elation. The relationship of plan area to height is important not just because of its spatial effect but because it is an important determinant of the ability of daylight to penetrate the space. It is frequently the case that the height required for the practical functioning of a space will not be sufficient to allow daylight to illuminate it properly: this is often observed in large open-plan offices where the limited floor-to-ceiling height limits daylight penetration and requires the use of permanent artificial lighting at a financial and environmental cost.

The importance of scale and proportion has been appreciated for millenia and has been the subject of much observation and theorising by architects, artists and thinkers anxious to discover and promote a universal system that would guarantee visual perfection in artefacts and buildings. These systems have ranged from the purely mathematical, such as that of the **Fibonacci Sequence** and the **Golden Section**, a proportioning system used by the ancient Greeks, to the proposal by Leonardo da Vinci that the reach and proportions of the human body be taken as a lodestone of design. In 1947 the great modernist

Swiss architect Le Corbusier proposed a system he titled **The Modulor** which incorporated both anthropometry and a mathematical proportioning system. It is difficult to be sure to what extent these systems were used as a part of the creative process and how much they are the result of a *post facto* analysis of existing, widely admired, designs focusing on such things as classical Greek temples and the volutes of seashells. It has to be said that, although interesting, the application of these ideas is hard to achieve in any complete and consistent way, not least because they are essentially two-dimensional constructs in a three-dimensional world. Of more practical, if prosaic, importance is the work that has been done to identify and record anthropometric data from contemporary societies. This information is invaluable in creating spaces, processes and products that are in accord with the proportions and movements of the human body.

Adolf Loos (Austria)

1870–1933

Notable projects:

Steiner House, Vienna, Austria

Müller House, Prague, Czech Republic

Karntner Bar, Vienna, Austria

Adolf Loos is often credited with the appearance of Modernist architectural design. He is perhaps better know for his ideas than his buildings, having been one of the first to argue against the use of superfluous decoration, establishing instead a building method supported by reason and necessity only. His writings and beliefs gave rise to the concept of 'Raumplan' or 'space-plan', an intricate three-dimensional organisation of space, where building design is thought of as a system of interlocking volumes, perfectly realised in the Moller House and Müller House. His fight for freedom from the decorative arts of the 1800s led the way for many twentieth-century architects and designers.

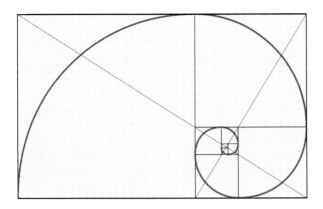

Golden Section

Dividing a line in the ratio 8:13 creates a situation where the relationship of the longer part to the shorter is virtually identical to the relationship of the longer part to the whole. This ratio was thought by the ancients to produce beautiful proportions. The ratio is very similar to that produced by the Fibonacci Sequence. Shapes defined by the Golden Section have been used by mankind for hundreds of years – its use may go back as far as the design of the Egyptian pyramids, Greek temples and the Renaissance. It continues to form the basis of much art, architecture, and design today.

0, 1, 1, 2, 3, 5, 8, 13, 21, 34, 55, 89, 144, 233, 377, 610, 987, 1597, 2584, 4181, 6765, 10946…

Fibonacci Sequence

A series of numbers where each is the sum of the preceding two, identified by Fibonacci (Leonardo of Pisa) in the Middle Ages and used as the basis of proportioning systems ever since. Proportions of this ratio are particularly pleasing to the eye and are commonly found in nature. As the series progresses, the ratio of a Fibonacci number divided by its predeccesor gets closer to 1.618: the Golden Section.

The Modulor

Devised by Le Corbusier and patented by him, the Modulor was the subject of his 1948 book, *Le Modulor.* Intended to be a harmonious scale applicable to architecture and engineering, it has seen widespread use in all aspects of the design industry. It uses the main proportions and dimensions of the human body in conjunction with the Golden Section, Fibonacci Sequence and a ratio of spatial distances to devise a system of measurements to be used when designing buildings and their interiors.

Charles Édouard Jeanneret Le Corbusier (Switzerland)

1887–1965
Notable projects:
Villa Savoye, Poissy, France
Perhaps the most influential figure in modern architecture, Le Corbusier developed a radical functionalist architecture of building and planning that made him one of the most regarded (and quoted) architects of the Modern Movement. His early work was heavily influenced by nature but he later utilised heavier, industrial styles, with bold colours, sculptural forms and harsh materials. His work drew much criticism internationally but he produced many town planning schemes with an emphasis on vehicular, pedestrian and functional zones. His project at Firminy, in France, has only recently been completed.

vista

The form of space is not simply defined by the requirements of one individual space. It is often the case that a number of spaces need to co-exist and that visual (and practical) links need to be incorporated between them and perhaps with the world outside. 'Vistas', a term borrowed from the vocabulary of the landscape designer, are devices often used to frame or extend the outlook from key viewpoints of grand houses and their grounds. The principle remains valid and is viable in buildings of all sizes and types. Indeed it could be argued that generating the illusion of space by creating a vista is one of the most valuable acts that a designer can undertake in a crowded urban environment. Such vistas may be part of a private internal world (the houses of Adolf Loos provide eloquent examples) or offer visual stimulus and opportunity within a public or semi-public domain (one thinks of railway termini and shopping malls). In each case the vista creates in the viewer a sense of possibility: a possibility that may be illusory or theatrical but which fulfils the desire for visual novelty and expansiveness.

Related to vista is the contemporary interest in linking internal and external spaces. Historically, buildings and their settings have often had a carefully considered relationship, but one where the building was intended to be seen as backdrop to the garden, or the garden seen as backdrop to the building. The houses designed by Edwin Lutyens with gardens by Gertrude Jekyll epitomise this approach. Recently this concept has been expanded by bringing the garden into the house, the house into the garden; blurring the line between the ending of one and the beginning of the other and treating the external space as a 'room' in its own right, with hard floor and semi-permanent furniture. This tendency has been characterised by foldaway walls and innovative use of glass structures; the latter probably spurred by the extraordinary glazed house extension created by Rick Mather Architects in 1992 that used glass for both structure and envelope.

Throughout history, designers have used form, proportion and vista to generate practical and delightful spaces, but there are other tools available to them. One of them is surprise. The public entrance to Vladislav Hall in Prague Castle is an ordinary door leading into a rather awkward antechamber of slightly depressing form and finish where admission tickets are sold. At the end of the antechamber is a very small, very ordinary door to which the ticket seller points the visitor. So far the experience has been distinctly underwhelming. Open that second door, however, and the result is stunning. The world explodes into space and light: an experience impossible to forget. Of course it is a trick: the same trick that is employed in film and television when the crocodile bursts out of the tranquil lagoon; the landmine explodes in the jungle clearing. The trick is to recognise the trick and to use it – sparingly and appropriately.

Richard Meier (USA)

1934
Notable projects:
Museum of Decorative Arts, Frankfurt, Germany
Barcelona Museum of Contemporary Art, Barcelona, Spain

Richard Meier has kept a constant style throughout his career. He is well known for his neo-modernist, purist designs for museums, residential and public spaces. Meier's work can be found worldwide and his buildings have received many awards. His designs resemble those of Le Corbusier, often making use of white planar elements with enamelled panels and glass. His use of ramps and handrails is also commonly found in examples of good, accessible interior and architectural design. His works have been popular throughout the 1980s, 1990s and the twenty-first century.

Hampstead House, kitchen (left)

Location: London, UK

Date: 2004

Designer: Blacksheep

The glazed extension to the rear of this kitchen articulates a relationship with the existing building, and also enables the designer to explore the threshold between interior and exterior space. This relationship is further expressed through the continuity of materials.

Photograph by Gareth Gardner, provided courtesy of Blacksheep

the fundamentals of interior architecture
SPACE/form

Hampstead House, dining area (left)

Location: London, UK

Date: 2004

Designer: Blacksheep

The dining space to this house in Hampstead is an independent environment, which is visually connected to the adjacent room. This impacts on our perception of the volume of this space in that it seems larger than it really is, whilst nevertheless limiting its actual size.

Photograph by Gareth Gardner, provided courtesy of Blacksheep

movement

We have already mentioned vista, an essentially static promise of future possibility. But the interior architect must not discount the potential of delight created by real movement through space. Routes within buildings may take many forms, but become especially interesting when they invoke all three dimensions. Stairs, ramps, escalators and lifts can all play their practical part in moving their users through space, but they can also simultaneously create possibilities of revelation and intrigue.

The stairs may be considered the most common of the three devices, but the physical form of the staircase offers huge possibilities – both as a sculpture in its own right and as a device for linking or counterpointing forms and materials on consecutive levels. The materials of which stairs can be made are marvels in themselves; the glass staircases created by the Czech engineer and architect Eva Jiricna should be valued as some of the wonders of our age.

Villa Arena Furniture Shopping Mall (left)
Location: Amsterdam, The Netherlands
Date: 2001
Designer: Virgile and Stone
The horizontal and vertical circulation through this shopping mall is key to the form and successful functioning of a large space. *Photograph courtesy of Virgile and Stone*

Zaha Hadid (Iraq)
1950
Notable projects:
Rosenthal Center for Contemporary Art, Ohio, USA
Vitra Fire Station, Weil am Rhein, Germany

Zaha Hadid became the first woman to win the Pritzker Prize for Architecture in 2004. Her designs are well known for their chaotic and modernist composition, often utilising fragmented geometry and multiple points of perspective to represent the chaos of modern-day life. Her work has been said to reject modernism, in the quest for a 'neo-modernism' that shatters rules of space such as ceilings, walls, front and back, and re-assembles them in an unconventional way. Her projects, found throughout the world, continue to push the boundaries of urban design and architecture. She has designed interiors as far afield as Hong Kong, Italy, Spain, USA, Denmark and Japan.
<www.zaha-hadid.com>

elements & composition of interior space

the fundamentals of interior architecture
SPACE/form

Le Corbusier claimed that 'a stair separates – a ramp connects', and it is certainly true that the ramp contains possibilities of flow and gentle transition that the fundamentally jerky movement (both visually and practically) of the staircase finds difficult to embody. Like all architectural devices the ramp has both pragmatic and aesthetic qualities that have been employed in different proportions for different reasons throughout history. The important point about ramps is that to be effortless in use they need to be shallow, but being shallow means that they need to be lengthy and it is often difficult in real-world situations to accommodate that length. In the case of Richard Meier, who has used ramps more consistently than any other contemporary architect, a significant proportion of the building volume is devoted to ramp access (look at the Museum of Contemporary Art in Barcelona and the Museum of Decorative Arts in Frankfurt). Many years earlier Frank Lloyd Wright had adopted a different approach when creating the Guggenheim Museum in New York by winding the ramp into a spiral around a hollow, cone-shaped void. In doing so he created a system that was both gallery space and access system and which, while presenting problems to exhibition curators ever since, created an iconic building.

Escalators and lifts work slightly differently. Glass lifts, particularly those climbing the external façade, are no longer a novelty but still have a powerful appeal. In many ways the escalator provides a composite of the experience of lift, ramp and stair because of its self-propelled trajectory; but so often the form and materials of the device itself and the awkward transition between human and mechanical propulsion at the beginning and end of the journey are less than satisfactory. However, here too glass is playing an increasing role in diminishing the slab-sided aspect of the traditional installation so that one hopes that in the not-too-distant future the sculptural form will achieve the refinement that it deserves.

'I strive for an architecture from which nothing can be taken away.'
Helmut Jahn

Frank Lloyd Wright (USA)
1867–1959
Notable projects:
Fallingwater, Pennsylvania, USA
Guggenheim Museum, New York, USA
Prairie House, New York, USA

A key figure in interiors, Lloyd Wright is frequently credited with instigating the move away from single-function, box-like room living to a more communal, shared space concept. Using simple materials, he experimented with screening devices, subtle changes in ceiling height and floating planar elements in order to do this. Wright practised what is known as organic architecture, making use of simple materials such as brick, wood and plaster. During his lifetime he was also instrumental in the move to begin protecting old buildings. The Frank Lloyd Wright Foundation now exists to conserve the work of the architect and advance the organic method of architecture and teaching that he promoted.

London Loft, staircase view (left)

Location: London, UK

Date: 2004

Designer: Jonathan Stickland

This staircase is not simply a functional device – it provides a strong sculptural focal point to the space.

Photograph by James Morris <www.jamesmorris.info>, provided courtesy of Jonathan Stickland

elements & composition of interior space

'All architecture is shelter, all great architecture is the design of space that contains, cuddles, exalts, or stimulates the persons in that space.'
Philip Johnson

transition

Of course much of the day-to-day movement in the buildings we use is from space to space, room to room, inside to outside. Pragmatically we only need a bit of corridor, or a doorway. But if we stop to consider what might be achievable rather than what we need, the possibilities become more interesting. Any space linking two others is a transitional preparation. This is not a negative space, but one capable of supporting its own character – an event in its own right. By thinking about the form, proportions, lighting and mood of that event we can make it a social space or an individual one, a portent of spaces to come or a reminder of things past. To do this we need to make decisions about the direction of travel and the sizes of openings. Should the user move directly or obliquely through the space?

Are doors necessary or could a screened opening achieve a more satisfactory result? Does opening a door provide the first, sudden, intimation of what is to come or does a carefully positioned aperture offer a preparatory hint? If a door is necessary is it something identifiably different from its surround, or is it an adjustable component of the wall that vanishes when closed and open and becomes an infinitely variable screen at positions in between? There are no predetermined answers to any of these questions; the potential solutions are answerable only to the context, the brief and the designer's conceptual approach, but it is in the exploration of these ideas that we begin to identify the difference between the activities of 'building' and 'interior architecture'.

MBAM (Marble Bar Asset Management) trading floor, view of corridor (left)

Location: London, UK

Date: 2004

Designer: Blacksheep

Transient environments operate on the threshold between spaces. Corridors are typical of such environments and serve to link together the different areas of an interior. Although corridors may be defined as secondary spaces they play an important role in the narrative of any given building.

Photograph by Francesca Yorke, provided courtesy of Blacksheep

the fundamentals of interior architecture
SPACE/form

'Architecture is basically a container of something. I hope they will enjoy not so much the teacup, but the tea.'
Yoshio Taniguchi

accessibility

Much of this chapter has been devoted to the spatial experience and to movement in the interior. This, of course, makes the assumption that the interior is accessible in the first place. Until comparatively recently buildings have been unthinkingly designed for that proportion of society which is strong, mobile and with good vision, completely discounting those – the young, the elderly and the disabled – for whom heavy doors, stairs, narrow openings and lack of visual contrast are a real barrier to their use. Tireless campaigning by the Helen Hamlyn Foundation and an awareness of the 'Design for Our Future Selves' work at the Royal College of Art have done much to bring these issues to the forefront of designer thinking and made building owners and the professions accepting of a responsibility to create accessibility and usability for all sectors of society. These responsibilities were enshrined in the Disability Discrimination Act of 1995 and are applicable to all new buildings and most rehabilitation work and must be seen as an opportunity to create good, inclusive, design that is accessible and enjoyable by the diverse components of modern society.

British Red Cross headquarters, interior view (facing page)

Location: London, UK

Date: 2005

Designer: Universal Design Studio

A sense of privacy is generated here without creating a separate room. The etched glass panels and screens enable degrees of privacy to be achieved whilst retaining some spatial continuity between the enclosure and the surrounding space.
Photograph courtesy of Universal Design Studio

elements & composition of interior space

questions in summary

elements & composition
of interior space

1 2 3 4

| What are the fundamental elements key to the creation of interior space? | How does the interior architect use walls, floors and ceilings? | How can an interior impart character and quality? | How do we perceive ourselves within a space? |

5 6 7 8

What role do external elements play in the composition of interior space?

How do we move within interior space?

Do devices such as doors play a role in the composition of interior space? If so, how?

How do we move between interior and exterior?

The interior architect never works in
the abstract. The host building and its
surroundings and the client's requirements
(as well as the need to respect building and
planning regulations) all define a contextual
framework within which the design must
exist. This framework will create both
potentials and restrictions. Although it
may seem counter-intuitive, it is often the
restrictions that allow the designer to
narrow down what would otherwise be
a bewildering array of design possibilities.
In order to appreciate the contextual
framework, one of the first tasks when
confronted with a new design commission
is to gain understanding of the host
building and its surrounding environment:
this applies whether it is a new building,
as yet invisible except as series of
drawings and models, or an existing
building that is being repurposed. This
understanding will be related to the building
and its function as it was, and will be
used to inform the design of the building
and its future function.

analysing the site

in this section

position / history / building typology / orientation / structure / services

The section that follows describes the issues that need to be appreciated in order that the designer has a proper understanding of the site. The word 'site' can be used in reference to the piece of land on which a building sits, or to describe the totality of the building and its location; encapsulating all the qualities that are currently present while at the same time acknowledging the variables brought about by time and change.

position

The architect will analyse a building in the context of its surroundings: assessing its relationship to existing routeways (pedestrian and vehicular), topography and its physical and visual connections with adjacent buildings. This is important in order to understand constraints and to identify possible noise sources, overlooking, shadow patterns, aesthetic links and access possibilities. Some of these things may be apparent from maps and photographs but it is essential to gain first-hand understanding and that means visiting the site; exploring both it and its surrounding area, not just once but a number of times under a range of different conditions. Environments and buildings change character from morning to evening, from weekday to weekend and from winter to summer, and it is important that these characteristics are recognised and then assimilated within the design process.

history

The building will have a physical position in its environment, but it will also have a social one. The latter is often made evident by its building typology (see page 48). Buildings that play an important social, religious or commercial role in society are designed and positioned in a way that makes them stand out from their surroundings and usually employ architectural forms and materials that are indicative of their importance. Churches, banks and government buildings are instantly recognised by their physical presence, and the materials from which they are built usually accentuate this. Reading some architectural histories one might be forgiven for thinking that only constructions having size and status deserve the term 'architecture' – everything else being simply 'building' – but even the humblest dwelling needs doors, walls, a roof and, usually, windows, and in the position and treatment of these can often be seen an aspirational echo of grander buildings and materials. As an example of the way these echoes track down through history, the modern Georgian-esque town house is itself an impoverished version of the eighteenth-century original that – with its vertical procession of semi-basement, raised ground floor, first floor reception room, bedroom floor and attics – reflected in miniature the vertical arrangement of grand country houses. The designer will not simply be concerned with the site as it is, but will want to understand the site as it was, in order to discover possible references for the design strategy. The building was created in a particular way to accommodate the needs of its first owner or user, and shaped to suit particular processes or activities. Since its creation a variety of changes may have modified its form and appearance. Some of those changes may have been brought about by the natural rhythm of human activity: environments that serve a particular need change and expand to meet that requirement, but ultimately are made redundant by new requirements and new processes that may adopt and adapt the original building. Other changes may be brought about by weathering or by natural or man-made disaster, others still by changes in technology and building practice that replace original materials and components with ones that are more effective, cheaper, or more readily available.

Some sites reflect a history of stable continuity, others of change and modification. Part of the interior architect's role is to recognise this history and develop a strategy that integrates the old with the new in a considered and productive relationship.

thinking about design 1.
The design process has been the subject of much scrutiny and debate over centuries. This fascination with the subject is partly due to the huge range of interacting demands and relationships that need to be resolved in every project. The number of variables to which the designer must attend is immense and incapable of resolution en masse. It is only by tackling them sequentially that we can deal with the complexities of the process. The chapter headings of this book – and, of course, the contents of the chapters – suggest topics that might be used in this sequential process.

Renzo Piano (Italy)
1937
Notable projects:
Centre Pompidou, Paris, France
Auditorium Parco della Musica, Rome, Italy
Renovation and expansion of Morgan Library, New York, US
Renzo Piano's work can be seen all over the world, from Australia and Japan to Germany and France. His projects range from apartments, shopping centres and factories, to bridges, boats and airport terminals. He is well known for his 'high-tech' designs, often using established technology as the starting point for building projects. Perhaps one of his most famous projects was the Pompidou Centre in Paris, France. This uses colour-coded service and structure elements on the exterior of the building and even the escalators are situated on the outside of the structure. The entire place, interior and exterior, is built to an 8mm grid.
<www.rpbw.r.ui-pro.com>

building typology

Building typology is a phrase that describes the architectural form, **construction** and original purpose of a building. Recognising and understanding these is essential in order to create a spatial, material and structural strategy for new interior work that will institute a **dialogue** with the existing building, which will be both cost-effective and safe. In order to do this an early part of any project is likely to be a detailed survey of the building. This survey will combine measured, structural and material information and is often one of the most useful tasks that a young designer can undertake at the beginning of a professional career. By looking closely at how things have been put together in the past, the designer acquires an understanding of materials, structural systems and fixings that can inspire the design decisions of the future and, more prosaically, ensure that there are no surprises when construction starts.

Looking at things as they are could be a very superficial process, concerned only with the immediately visible surfaces and edges. It is important that the designer appreciates and learns to recognise the underlying materials and structures on which the visible surface depends. Some building types are so monolithic that what appears on the surface is an accurate representation of the intrinsic structure of the building, while in others the structural layering of the building is invisible to the casual observer and requires understanding and experience on the part of that observer in order to decipher it. The ability to recognise and 'read' this information is an important skill.

thomascook.com, office fit-out, external view (above)

Location: Peterborough, UK

Date: 2001

Designer: Bluebottle

This is an example of a building type the designer may need to utilise. This contemporary 'shed' has no historical detail to inform the design process, but the nature of its construction means that it is a flexible and adaptable space with which to work.

Photograph by Nathan Willock, provided courtesy of Bluebottle

construction

The placement and interrelationship of structural elements.

dialogue

The word dialogue is used in everyday speech to mean a verbal interchange between people. In the language of design the same word is used to describe the practical or sensory interaction between the components of a scheme.

orientation

Orientation is important to the interior for two reasons: the position of the building in relation to the path of the sun is the key to making best use of the available daylight and sunlight, and orientation also determines the way that the building is perceived in its surroundings and the views that can be achieved of those surroundings.

Few buildings, particularly those in urban surroundings, are positioned to take best advantage of available light. The principle positional determinant is more likely to be that provided by the relationship with the street pattern and, perhaps, other key buildings. The pressures of social standing decree that the street façade of the building is the one that heralds the values and aspirations of the architect, builder and owner, expressing these values in terms of composition and in the use of materials. Historically, glass was an expensive material that, when used extensively in the front façade, denoted the status of the building and the affluence of its owner. As compensation, the back of the building, hidden from public view, was very often less generously glazed, irrespective of which of the elevations were best-placed to take advantage of available light.

It is often the case that in old or much-modified buildings, the existing spaces make poor use of natural light. In such cases part of the design strategy may be to re-organise them to redress this shortcoming – perhaps by changing the form or position of the spaces themselves, perhaps by 'borrowing' light by creating openings.

The close relationship between light and colour will be discussed in a later chapter. The effects of orientation may extend to affecting the choice of colour for internal spaces: for instance colours in the red or yellow part of the spectrum might be employed in north-facing spaces to counter the lack of direct sunlight and to help create the illusion of warmth.

Stella McCartney UK flagship store, view of conservatory (left)

Location: London, UK
Date: 2002
Designer: Universal Design Studio

The extension to this store in London is constructed almost entirely of glass. Not only does this enable the space to retain the same amount of natural light that already enters the courtyard, it creates a relatively 'invisible' structure within the space, thus avoiding compromising the availability of light to the surrounding environment.

Photograph by Richard Davies, provided courtesy of Universal Design Studio

analysing the site

structure

For most designers, the structural systems that they will discover and employ are likely to be variations on (or hybrids of) a limited number of structural types.

For buildings before c.1920 (with the exception of certain large-span spaces such as railway stations) the preponderant systems will be **loadbearing wall** or **post-and-beam** structures. These structures are typified by the use of identifiably separate components for the horizontal (floors) and vertical (walls or posts) elements of the building. The result of this separation is that there is little structural continuity within the building, making such systems structurally inefficient in modern terms. This inefficiency means that the structural elements themselves are comparatively massive and thus have a significant visual and spatial effect on the internal environment. These systems remain widely employed today in small-scale, particularly residential, buildings. They have the benefit of being easily understood and assembled by any competent tradesman and are, as long as their principles are properly appreciated, very amenable to modification.

Loadbearing wall and post-and-beam structures tend to create spaces that are limited in width and in which the structural elements are dominant. They are not necessarily small buildings. The Parthenon in Athens (built c.475 BC) is a good example of a large building using post-and-beam principles. John Onians has suggested that the forest of columns that dominates the Parthenon's interior space was understood by the ancient Greeks as a reference to the protective power of a phalanx of soldiers; but it is probably also true that, with the materials and techniques available, such a large building could have been built in no other way at that time.

The structural systems identified above continue to be used. However, since c.1930 increasing use has been made of **frame** or **column-and-slab** systems where the beams and supporting columns (and in the case of column-and-slab buildings the floors themselves) are integrated in a steel, or steel-reinforced concrete, construction system. Structurally this is much more efficient than the separate components of the loadbearing wall or post-and-beam systems, meaning that the floors themselves can be shallower and the supporting columns more widely spaced. These systems are widespread in commercial work (shops, offices, factories) but, partly because of their superior acoustic and fire performance, are increasingly found in medium and large-scale residential work. Such systems are capable of modification, but require careful structural analysis and the employment of specialist contractors.

loadbearing wall	post-and-beam	frame	column-and-slab
A wall that supports other parts of the structure. Often made of stone, brick or concrete.	A structure that uses a frame of uprights and horizontal beams.	A skeleton structure of steel or steel-reinforced concrete, which provides the strength and stability of the building, independent of walls or floors. Timber may be used to provide the framing of small buildings.	A building system in which steel-reinforced concrete is used to create an integrated structural system of great strength and stiffness.

Besom Trust, existing site (left)

Location: London, UK

Date: 2006

Designer: Blacksheep

The marrying of new structural inserts with the existing structure is thoughtfully articulated here. Note the brick column in particular, which has been carefully made, suggesting that it will be left as it is rather than being concealed by applied materials and finishes.

Photograph courtesy of Blacksheep

SITE/function

These systems offer much greater freedom to the interior structure, allowing internal walls to be placed for maximum efficiency and effect. At the same time the stiffness of the joint between vertical and horizontal components potentially frees the external wall of any structural role, permitting it to be more responsive to requirements of daylight and vista.

The four structural systems described thus far may be used for multi-storey buildings. For some types of building however, the provision of a column-free space is the paramount requirement. Aircraft hangars, railway stations, places of worship and assembly and sports stadiums all need clear sightlines and access. Various forms of lattice frame and shell structures that create a weatherproof envelope over a single volume can meet these needs. The smallest form of shell structure is probably the igloo (although, strictly speaking, this only becomes a true shell structure as the snow blocks integrate with use and time: when first built it is a loadbearing wall structure!); larger shell structures have been built using a variety of materials – metals, concrete and plastic – witness the biomes created for the Eden project in Cornwall and the expressive forms of the Sydney Opera House.

Scottish Spa, roof detail (right)

Location: Isle of Islay, UK

Date: 2006

Designer: Jonathan Stickland

Although this building looks like a traditional stone barn it is in fact a brand new building. The use of stone is complemented by the timber roof trusses, which sit happily alongside the more obviously 'contemporary' elements of the scheme. Hence the slate floor sits beautifully alongside the pristine white walls and the timber trusses frame the space.

Photograph courtesy of Jonathan Stickland

Scottish Spa, swimming pool (facing page)

Location: Isle of Islay, UK

Date: 2006

Designer: Jonathan Stickland

The previous aesthetic is continued in the detailing of this structure. Note the use of a steel plate to link the concrete ring beam with the timber roof member, making a clean, precise connection.

Photograph courtesy of Jonathan Stickland

London Loft, view of bathroom (above)

Location: London, UK

Date: 2004

Designer: Jonathan Stickland

This extensive bathroom has cabling to the lighting, a plasma screen television and extraction fan as well as hot and cold water supplies and drainage pipes to basins and tub. These have been carefully integrated within the construction so that they are invisible.

Photograph by James Morris <www.jamesmorris.info>, provided courtesy of Jonathan Stickland

thinking about design 2.

Unconscious design can be more effective than conscious. There is often the hope that consciously deliberating on a problem will trigger a creative solution. In the case of simple problems this will often work (when reassembling a piece of machinery for instance, or solving an anagram). For complex problems, particularly those combining practical and aesthetic solutions, there is a better way. That better way is unconscious deliberation; using the parallel processing power of the brain to solve the problem subconsciously while the brain's owner embarks on another task. The only proviso is that the brain has to understand all the variables and their relationships before it can work this particular magic; this means there has to be an initial conscious effort to feed it the right information. Afterwards the individual can get on with other things knowing that in the near future, often suddenly and in unlikely situations, a potential solution will occur.

services

Water, electricity, gas, drainage and heating and ventilation systems all fall under the heading of services. These things are important not just because of their effect on the functioning and comfort of the building but because the routing of wires, pipes and trunking that serves them needs to be taken into account in the layout of the interior. Unless an industrial aesthetic is intrinsic to the design concept, these things are better hidden – not just for visual reasons but as a means of protecting them from damage – and that requires some understanding of the sizes, connections and geometries that are required.

Supply cables and pipes can often be hidden within floor systems; but it is when they are required to travel vertically between floors or to supply fittings or equipment mounted on walls that the problems begin. Where the wall is to be plastered it is usual to cut a channel in the underlying wall, clip the pipes or cable in position and rely on plaster to hide the installation. It becomes more difficult on a fair-faced wall, where the brickwork, blockwork or stonework is intended to be seen without a covering of plaster or render. In such cases every effort should be taken to avoid wall-mounted components. Where they are unavoidable it is sometimes possible to run the supply on the other side, connecting via a hole drilled through the thickness of the wall. If that is not feasible then the only option is to express the installation as a design feature or conceal it with a cover plate or boxing.

Drainage pipes are the most disruptive elements, both because of their size and the fact that they need to run either vertically or at a shallow slope. For this reason it is good practice to cluster together facilities requiring water supply and drainage: either back-to-back (so that, for instance, a kitchen might back on to a shower room on the other side of a dividing wall) or stacked vertically (a bathroom on the floor level above a kitchen). In this way the service elements can be concentrated in one location, reducing the number of problems to be solved.

analysing the site

questions in summary
analysing the site

1 2 3 4

How does the surrounding environment affect the interior?

What role does history play in the reinvention of interior space?

How does position affect the interior?

What methods of construction will the interior architect be working with?

5 6

What restrictions do structural systems place on the design of interior space?

How can the interior architect incorporate heating, drainage, water, electricity and gas supply elements into the design of the interior?

the fundamentals of interior architecture
SITE/function

types of interior

in this section

retail spaces / work spaces / living spaces / public spaces / restorative spaces / transient spaces

For every occasion that a clear categorisation can be applied there will be others where the boundaries are blurred or where the design brief encompasses more than one category. What matters is that the designer has a clear understanding of the functional needs of the project and the creative vision to ensure that these can be fulfilled in a way that will create the appropriate emotional response in the building's user.

retail spaces
shops, banks, showrooms, restaurants & bars

The retail sector provides considerable work for the interior architecture profession. In part this work will be to do with the practicalities of display and selling, but on some occasions, the interior architect will have a role to play in re-branding an existing business or establishing the brand values for a new one. This work demands that the designer not only understands the values and aspirations of the company, but has a real understanding of the way that materials, colours and forms are perceived by society in general and the target market in particular, coupled with knowledge of the issues and costs involved in their use. The Apple Stores in New York and London, both implementations of the 'Apple Digital Lifestyle Concept' are in contrast to the same cities' 'NikeTowns'. The first are cool, technical exercises in metals and glass, the second gritty renderings of the urban experience. Both are perfect demonstrations of their respective company's brand values and identity, and examples of clear briefs meticulously pursued.

**Stella McCartney US
flagship store (right)**

Location: New York, USA

Date: 2002

Designer: Universal
Design Studio

The design of retail
environments can bring into
play theatrical devices – note
the quality of light in particular
here. The relative
impermanence of these types
of spaces enables the designer
to explore form, texture and
light in ways that capture the
imagination of the user. These
are places to shop and to
make believe.

*Photograph by Frank
Oudeman, provided courtesy of
Universal Design Studio*

the fundamentals of interior architecture
SITE/function

The selling environment will require **display** space that is reflective of the **brand values** of the business; one that is easy to stock and able to present the product to the customer in an inviting way. An understanding of **ergonomics**, **anthropometrics** (which of us has not struggled to reach products, or read information, on shelving too high or too low for comfort?) and lighting (see chapter 4) will be required, as will an active consideration for the comfort and security of the customers and staff.

Choice of materials will have a significant effect both on perceptions of quality and on the acoustic ambience of retail spaces. A large group of people in a social setting will produce a significant amount of noise and this will need to be factored into the choice of materials. Hard materials – metals, ceramic, plaster, plastic laminates – will create an acoustically 'bright' environment. Whether the ambience created by such acoustics is regarded as cheap-and-cheerful or

dynamic and sophisticated will depend on the quality, finish and colours of the materials chosen and the contribution of such secondary elements as choice of furniture and, particularly, the expectation triggered by the food or product offering and service. As an example, hard surfaces are intrinsic to the fast food outlet of the global high street, just as they are to Les Grandes Marches Restaurant in Paris (designed by Elisabeth de Portzamparc), but there is no possibility of mistaking the one for the other.

While hard materials will create bright acoustics, the same number of people in a carpeted, heavily curtained and soft-furnished space will experience the muted, respectful ambience redolent of traditional gentlemen's clubs and restaurants. Neither atmosphere is intrinsically better than the other, but each requires understanding and conscious decision-making to create a match with the brief and values of the client.

display
When working with clients in the retail sector, the interior architect's job, essentially, is to provide a space in which the client's product and brand will be displayed in an appropriate and effective manner.

brand values
All commercial organisations are focused on building and maintaining their business by identifying their target customer and ensuring that the company and the product are perceived as matching the personal standards and aspirations of the customer.

ergonomics
The study of the body's response to physical and physiological loads and strains. It is concerned with such things as safe weight limits, the effects of repetition, the application of force and the effects of posture.

anthropometrics
'The measurement of humans'. Statistical data about the distribution of body dimensions in the population used to optimise human interaction design decisions.

Burberry Milan flagship store (left)

Location: Milan, Italy

Date: 2002

Designer: Virgile and Stone

A crisp, clean-lined interior that reflects company values and demonstrates the merchandise effectively.

Photograph by Matteo Piazza, provided courtesy of Virgile and Stone

work spaces
offices, workshops, studios, factories

Work spaces, more than any other, are likely to be process-driven: that is they will be organised to suit the sequence, mode of work and philosophy of the operation they house. That does not mean that they have to be clinical, soulless spaces; very often an interior architect is employed to ensure that the quality of the activity and the values of the company are reflected in the appearance of the space. Look at the work done for advertising agency, Mother, by Clive Wilkinson Architects to see an example of a workplace that embodies strong identity within a dynamic work environment.

The steady increase of service activity as a proportion of the global economy has created a parallel interest in the provision of attractive and individualised workplaces. In modern business it is recognised that a healthy, alert workforce is good for profit as well as good for the individual. This recognition has led to a move away from the traditional hierarchical, often stratified, arrangement that encouraged a sedentary acceptance of role and position. Instead, there has been a move towards the creation of new types of places that encourage a more collegiate and collaborative approach to work. This ethos has been extended by the inclusion of exercise and relaxation zones in close proximity to the workstation. In turn these zones have generated ancillary spaces that support them: showers and changing facilities for users of the exercise facilities and for those who cycle to work, kitchens and food stores to support catering for coffee bars and restaurants. These all need to be factored into the design.

'I love building spaces: architecture, furniture, all of it, probably more than fashion.'
Donna Karan

Thomas Cook, Accoladia, office fit-out, interior view (left)

Location: Peterborough, UK

Date: 2001

Designer: Bluebottle

Strong geometrical forms and careful use of bold, contrasting colours create a dynamic-looking working environment. *Photograph by Frans Burrows, provided courtesy of Bluebottle*

types of interior

Not all design work will be done for corporate clients. The growth of telecommunications and niche employment has led to an increase in home working. Where space is available the home office or studio may be contained in a separate room behind a closed door. For many urban dwellers this is not an option and a more imaginative approach is needed if the living space is not to be overwhelmed by the work facility: a constant reminder of work not yet done. Various forms of storage wall and flexible division have been created to solve this problem. The home office produced within a modest Manhattan apartment for graphic designer Wing Chan by Roger Hirsch and Myriam Corti is a particularly elegant solution. Folding panels when opened reveal two work positions complete with computers and peripherals, filing cabinets and storage, but when closed create a living space of almost Miesian calm.

thinking about design 3.

Design problems cannot be solved entirely in the head. When a potential solution arrives as a result of conscious or unconscious thought, there is always the temptation to relax and to assume the job is finished. It won't be. When an idea arrives in the brain it must be externalised – got out of the brain – by translating it into a drawing or a model in order that the conscious brain can assess its value and determine whether it does indeed fulfill the appropriate criteria. There is every chance that it will not be quite as perfect a solution as it had seemed to be. Once its shortcomings are appreciated the designer can embark on another cycle of the iterative process and a refinement of the solution.

'We have to replace beauty, which is a cultural concept, with goodness, which is a humanist concept.' Philippe Starck

Gerrit Rietveld (The Netherlands)

1888–1964
Notable projects:
Schröder House, Utrecht, The Netherlands

Born in Holland, Rietveld was a founder member of the de Stijl group. A furniture-maker by trade, Rietveld produced a broad body of work, but it is his early output for which he is retrospectively appreciated. The Red Blue chair utilised the primary colours and orthogonal forms of a Mondrian painting but was structurally significant in the way that the seating and framing components were differentiated. His most influential project was the house built for Truus Schröder-Schräder in Utrecht in 1924. This used sliding partitions to create a space that, apart from a service core of bathroom, stove and staircase, could be configured in different ways to adapt to different needs. Extensive glazing provided views across what was then open farmland, at the same time accentuating the planar qualities of floor, ceiling and wall components. The house used a Mondrianesque palette of primary colours, together with white grey and black.

thomascook.com, office fit-out, interior view (left)

Location: Peterborough, UK

Date: 2001

Designer: Bluebottle

In order to create a separation between open-plan office space and private meeting areas, this interior describes a hierarchy of functions. Everyday activities take place at the lower level whilst more specialist needs are accommodated within the raised cubes, which overlook the communal environment.
Photograph by Nathan Willock, provided courtesy of Bluebottle

thomascook.com, view of office fit-out (left)

Location: Peterborough, UK

Date: 2001

Designer: Bluebottle

This scheme uses a new insertion in an existing building shed. There is an interesting separation between public and semi-public spaces here, with only the entirely private activities being contained within 'rooms'. Note the use of gabions for the feature wall – normally used in landscaping projects, the internalising of this 'exterior' architectural device emphasises the idea of creating a building within a building, and further articulates a relationship between the public face and behind-the-scenes functioning of this well known company.
Photograph by Nathan Willock, provided courtesy of Bluebottle

types of interior

living spaces
residential buildings, hotel accommodation

We tend to think of living spaces as epitomising very personal environments in which the individual can have a great degree of control over layout, furnishings and visual qualities. Although this may be true of private houses and apartments there are living spaces in hotels, hostels, and care homes where the interior architect will be providing a universal, rather than personal, solution. Whichever category is being designed for, the needs of comfort, consideration of furniture layouts, the disposition of facilities one to another, the enjoyment of light and view and the provision of adequate storage will all be part of the designer's agenda.

'Space and light and order. Those are the things that men need just as much as they need bread or a place to sleep.'
Le Corbusier

Philippe Starck (France)

1949
Notable projects:
Royalton Hotel, New York, USA
St Martins Lane Hotel, London, UK

Philippe Starck is one of the best-known designers of today, not only for his interior and architectural designs, but also for his product design. His work has sometimes been criticised for its strong bond with fashion and novelty but the twenty-first century seems to have seen a move closer to longevity and durability. Unlike many other designers, Starck does not concentrate on expensive single pieces, but instead produces usable household items, which can be marketed for mass production. His designs are known for their unusual combinations of materials and can be found throughout the world. One of his most notable projects, St Martin's Lane Hotel in London, UK, saw Starck transform the former home of a major advertising company into an exclusive boutique hotel. His use of colour, light and texture ensures that guests enjoy an exciting journey through various spaces during their stay.
<www.philippe-starck.com>

Pembridge Villas, interior view (above)

Location: London, UK

Date: 2001

Designer: Universal Design Studio

The strong geometric elements that comprise this interior are emphasised through the flooding of the space with natural light. The rectilinear skylight and door openings, which admit this light, both echo the shape of the space and further sculpt the interior into a geometric pattern of light and solid form.

Photograph courtesy of Universal Design Studio

SITE/function

Over the past forty years there has been intense interest in the reinvention of the private home. Inspiring buildings have been created, both in rural and urban settings. Many of these are new-builds, but it is the opportunity to transform existing, perhaps obsolete, buildings that holds most interest for the interior architect. Warehouses, churches, farm and manufacturing buildings have all been employed as the containers into which creative energy has been poured and from which novel and exciting spaces for living have emerged. The traditional house has not been immune to these forces and much has been done to create contemporary living solutions within the (sometimes extended) shell of domestic buildings that were originally designed and built for a very different society. It is worth looking at the work of Pierre d'Avoine for examples of sensitive re-working of existing buildings and for his insights into the possibilities for infill architecture in urban environments.

In a world in which the established hotel chains were endemic, the modern, one-off hotel received special attention with the creation of the Royalton Hotel, designed by Philippe Starck, on 44th Street, New York. A compelling mix of hard edges, high-luminance colour and hushed luxury, the hotel succeeded by attention to detail. Since then the number of custom-made hotels has burgeoned, one of the most recent being The Hotel Duomo in Rimini by Ron Arad, which uses seamless materials and invisible fixings to create interiors of great clarity and a sense of airiness.

Yoo Building Penthouse, snug entrance (right)

Location: London, UK

Date: 2004

Designer: Blacksheep

The 'snug' in this penthouse apartment does not function in the same way as any of the other spaces here. It is designed to be an intimate, private space, which is deliberately inaccessible. Rather like a tree-house or loft this is a secret space, which although occupying the same physical location, exists rather as a parallel space, sitting outside of the everyday functioning of the domestic environment.

Photograph by Gareth Gardner, provided courtesy of Blacksheep

thinking about design 4.

Design is a time-constrained activity. Since most designers are perfectionists there is a reluctance to accept a less than optimal solution to any problem. The reality of commercial design is that there will always be deadlines and these impose a restriction on the time that can be devoted to a problem. In order to get the best possible solution within the limited time available it is important that every designer understands their working process and the circumstances that allow them to carry out that process most efficiently. This means understanding the time of day, the facilities and the environmental variables – light, temperature, acoustics and air quality – that produce the most effective work.

public spaces

*airports, railway & bus stations, cinemas &
theatres, museums & galleries, religious buildings*

The layout of these spaces, often large in scale and required to accommodate great numbers of people, can be seen to have parallels with town planning. There is need for directed movement (streets), display and merchandising activity (the market square), zones of relaxation (cafés and seating) all laid out in an accessible and understandable manner. While it is unlikely that the interior architect will be responsible for the creation of the buildings themselves, there is work to be done in creating or renovating the facilities that they contain.

These facilities will vary in scale, both in themselves and in relation to the building envelope. One of the most difficult design tasks is to express a sense of identity and purpose for small facilities in large spaces. Transport and religious buildings tend to be majestic in scale and with very strong architectural identities. To create a facility that is neither overwhelmed by its context nor disruptive of it is a difficult balancing act and requires design of great integrity.

While it is unlikely that an interior architect will be in a position to design a church or an airport terminal, there are lessons to be learnt about the use of light and the formation of space from good examples of those buildings. Le Corbusier's Pilgrim Chapel (Notre Dame du Haut) at Ronchamp and Tadao Ando's Church of Light near Osaka and, at a vastly greater scale, Richard Rogers Partnership's Terminal 4 at Barajas Airport, Madrid, all employ sculptural form and a powerful use of light to create iconic spaces.

At a smaller and more enclosed scale the Virgin Atlantic Heathrow Clubhouse Lounge by the Virgin in-house design team and Softroom uses Eames loungers, hand-blocked wallpaper, leather-wrapped balustrades and sculptural seating and ceiling forms to create an environment that, while having some of the values of a gentlemen's club, is slick, open and modern.

Turbine Hall A, Battersea Power Station, computer image (right)

Location: London, UK

Date: 2008 (projected)

Designer: Universal Design Studio

This computer-generated visual illustrates a proposal for the interior of Battersea Power Station. It suggests how human activities and scale will be contained within the enormous space of the original structure. *Image courtesy of Universal Design Studio*

types of interior

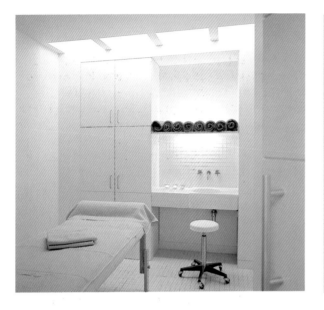

thinking about design 5.
It seems inevitable that there comes a point on every project when the design process slows to a halt. When this happens it is tempting to assume that there has been a shortcoming in the initial idea and to start again with a new concept. So long as the original problem was properly understood this is unlikely to be successful. All designs have to be worked at, remembering that it is not the concept that defines the design but the way that the concept is developed and resolved.

Space NK Spa NK (above)

Location: London, UK

Date: 2000

Designer: Virgile and Stone

This treatment room for Space NK is finished in cold, hard materials, which are then softened through the controlled use of light. The clinical feel to this space matches its function precisely.
Photograph by Chris Gascoigne, provided courtesy of Virgile and Stone

Rem Koolhaas (The Netherlands)

1944

Notable projects:

Kunsthal, Rotterdam, The Netherlands

Rem Koolhaas is a controversial figure in interiors and architecture: many have struggled to define his work and some have criticised it for its apparent lack of aesthetic concern. Koolhaas's designs seem to have little visual logic, often made up of seemingly unrelated and abstract visual forms. It seems, instead, to be more concerned with the social and technological elements of today's society, often exemplified by the use of ramps and easily accessible spaces in many of his works. He began his career as a writer and journalist, which earned him a reputation before he had even designed a building. He founded the OMA (Office for Metropolitan Architecture) in 1975, along with Elia Zenghelis, Zoe Zenghelis and Madelon Vriesendorp in London, UK. One of Koolhaas's students, Zaha Hadid, later joined them although she later went on to achieve much in the world of architecture independently. His work earned him the Pritzker Architecture Prize in 2000.

restorative spaces
hospitals, clinics, spas, gymnasiums

This category encompasses buildings of a great variety of sizes, from small health centres and spas to the mega-structures that are modern hospitals. Some of them are places that one visits only when necessary, others may be a part of the industry that has grown up around health, well-being and body-shaping. What is common to all of them is the need for an atmosphere that fits the narrative and image of both the facility and the client. This atmosphere may be evoked in any number of ways: by generating quiet spaces of Zen-like tranquillity at one extreme to creating powerful environments of such positivity that troubling thoughts are given no opportunity to develop at the other.

Whether it is a dental clinic or a gymnasium, a hospital clinic or a thermal spa, none of these are single-space events. They all take their users on a journey that starts at the street door (in reality even earlier) through a procession of events and activities before delivering them, in an improved condition, back to the outside world. Each of those events or activities will have its own needs and agenda, but most importantly, act as preparation for the core event. It is easy to give names to the spaces that these events and activities will inhabit – reception, changing room, waiting room – but the role of the designer is to explore what these events might mean, and the way they might fit, in the overall narrative. From this understanding, appropriate forms will be created and appropriate materials chosen.

The dental clinic on Kurfürstendamm in Berlin designed by Graft Architects is a good example of a designed response to the range of activity and the reinvention of practice that the economic pressures of modern dental care has created. Not just a series of treatment rooms served by a waiting space, the practice contains, amongst other things, a dental laboratory, a coffee/Internet lounge and a homeopathic surgery, all rendered as a sinuous, sculpted, bright orange experience that is at once welcoming and stimulating.

Charles and Ray Eames (USA)

1907, 1912
Notable projects:
Etenza House, California, USA
Lounge chair wood

Not only did Charles (1907-1978) and his wife Ray (1912-1988) produce some of the most iconic furniture of the twentieth century (licensed reproductions of which are still available) they also designed and built one of the twentieth century's most iconic houses in which they lived and worked. In addition they produced children's toys, films and exhibitions. Early experiments in formed plywood were followed by glassfibre, plastics and aluminium – each led to ranges of furniture and products. The house in Pacific Palisades, a suburb of Los Angeles, used off-the-shelf industrial components to produce a speedily-erected low-cost steel building characterised by primary-coloured panels and sliding walls and windows. Their zeal for design and their celebration of the everyday, as well as the precious, was communicated in a series of talks, writings and films. The Eames's work has come to represent the USA's defining social movement: the coming-of-age of the West Coast and the expansion of American culture. <www.eamesoffice.com>

transient spaces
exhibition & display

All interior architecture is affected by the trends and pressures of fashion, but probably none more so than exhibition and display design. Whether it is for a travelling museum exhibition or a company stand for a trade fair, the role of the designer is to capture the attention and to display and promote the artefact or information. This needs to be done in a fresh and original way that is consistent with the exhibited object and, in the case of a trade stand, the values of the company. While a travelling museum exhibition may be seen only once by any individual, trade stands need to attract the corporate client consistently time and again and to do so need to be constantly reinvented. To achieve this requires an understanding of marketing strategy coupled with architectural creativity.

Some of these spaces are effectively miniature buildings (witness the stands created for Sto by Arno Design), others more abstract and sculptural in form (Totems Architecture's stand for the German engineering company Bertrand), yet others defy convention and expectation by engaging with the user in unusual ways (the Perception Restrained exhibition at MoMA New York by Herzog & de Meuron), but all capture the attention and stimulate the imagination.

Crafts Council exhibition, 'Beauty and the Beast: New Swedish Design', 'Beauty' gallery, detail of display (right)

Location: London and Manchester, UK

Date: 2004–05

Designer: Nick Coombe

The low-level plinths that house the objects on display here re-create their original domestic context. It is interesting to note that the geometry of the display plinths was derived from that of the exhibits (e.g. the side of an Ingegerd Rahmen bowl), but at 50 times the original scale.

Photograph by James Morris <www.jamesmorris.info>, provided courtesy of Nick Coombe

Crafts Council exhibition, 'Beauty and the Beast: New Swedish Design', general view of 'Beauty' gallery (facing page)

Location: London and Manchester, UK

Date: 2004–05

Designer: Nick Coombe

The forms and layout of this exhibition display allude to the domestic setting for which the products are intended.

Photograph by James Morris <www.jamesmorris.info>, provided courtesy of Nick Coombe

types of interior

questions in summary
types of interior

1 2 3 4

What sort of spaces might the interior architect need to work with?

How might the interior architect design a space for clients in the retail sector?

What factors are important in the design of space in a working environment?

How does the interior architect work with residential and hotel accommodation?

5 6 7

How does the interior architect create a space that is suitable for public use?

How can the interior architect create a space that is calming and at the same time functional?

How might the interior architect be involved in creating a space for exhibition and display?

The form of the host building, discussed in the last chapter, is made visible by the materials of which it is constructed and in which it is finished. As individuals we are able, both consciously and unconsciously, to appreciate the qualities of space, but it is the materials, textures and colours used in that space to which we ultimately relate. Part of this is a visual relationship, but often this relationship is a product of a sense of recognition: of previous experiences of those materials and finishes, the contexts in which they were encountered and of their tactile, acoustic and light-modifying qualities. These associations provide the designer with an opportunity to offer visual and tactile cues about the building, its quality and purpose while simultaneously providing the chance to subvert expectations and to create intrigue and excitement by employing materials and finishes in unexpected ways and in unusual combinations.

understanding the interior

in this section

integral elements / introduced elements

Every element of the interior environment is susceptible to conscious and considered decision making. This means understanding those elements that are integral to the existing building fabric and making decisions about their preservation, alteration and treatment, while also considering those elements that will be introduced into the designed environment as part of the project strategy. Incorporated in both these categories, there is a very wide range of scales.

integral elements

The integral elements, the interior fabric, will define the volumetric space, or spaces, within which the interior architect will operate. The materials and construction of the fabric will be a legacy of the style and purpose of the original building and of its subsequent history. This points to one of the abiding issues in interior architecture. It was identified in the introduction that the reuse and repurposing of existing buildings is a key aspect of the interior architecture discipline. Every existing building comes with a history of change overlain on the background of its original form and style and it is incumbent on the designer to recognise what is valuable in that legacy and design in such a way as to respond to it. This applies as much to materials as it does to forms and volumes.

The Society for the Protection of Ancient Buildings, a society founded by William Morris in 1877 at a time when there was concern for the survival of the British architectural legacy, holds as one of its tenets that the changes that have occurred over time are as valuable to the building as its original form and fabric, and should be recognised and respected as such.

Irish pavilion, Hanover Expo 2000 (left)

Location: Hanover, Germany

Date: 2000

Designer: Dul Consortium

The use of gabions to construct this pavilion for the Hanover Expo in 2000, expresses the 'idea' of the Irish landscape within the materiality of the structure. Materials themselves can contain meaning and thus the choice of materials in any interior space should be an extension of the overall conceptual approach.

Photograph courtesy of Jonathan Mortimer

MATERIALS/texture

Hampstead House, view of kitchen extension (above)
Location: London, UK

Date: 2004

Designer: Blacksheep

There is a combination of old and new materials at play here. The existing brickwork of the early twentieth-century house is bisected by the clean lines of the glazed extension. The solid timber furniture will also weather gracefully over time.

Photograph by Gareth Gardner, provided courtesy of Blacksheep

Alvar Aalto (Finland)
1898–1976

Notable projects:

Riola Parish Church, Riola, Italy

Alvar Aalto's work has been particularly significant in interior architecture due to its exceptional form and planning and response to site and material. Aalto's composed style, which embraces functialism and expressionism in a uniquely sensual fashion, has lent itself well to his designs of buildings such as libraries and churches, as well as residential developments. Aalto's furniture and architectural designs are celebrated throughout the world, as well as in his native Finland, and his understanding of people as a part of the diversity and complexity of nature is in complete harmony with and of growing importance to the new ecological attitude towards design today.

This is a precept that remains useful today. Few buildings survive through time in their original state: they are modified and extended to suit need and fashion and part of their fascination and character is a result of these changes. Since every addition represents an investment of time and money, it makes financial as well as ethical sense to acknowledge and retain such changes where possible, but, as is always the case in design, there are no absolutes and the designer needs to weigh up the options. In some situations retention of the historical legacy, in others a stripping away of the accumulations, may be the appropriate response.

The building style and character are created not just by the major elements of walls, ceilings and floors and of the materials of which they are made, but will also include smaller, more detailed elements: doors and windows for instance, their fastenings, handles and hinges, as well as **architraves** and **skirtings**. These things might seem like trivial adjuncts to the building structure, but their presence is essential to the character of certain building styles that can look bereft if they are removed.

architrave

The element, often a timber moulding, that masks the joint between the door or window frame and an adjacent wall surface. In traditional construction the first being made of timber, the second of plaster, there will always be a crack between these surfaces – a crack accentuated by the slamming of the door or window. With careful detail design and choice of materials it is possible to minimise or eliminate this component.

skirting

The cover strip that runs at the bottom of the wall and abuts the floor. As with the architrave this is a device for reconciling two dissimilar materials. It also provides a tough surface intended to resist the impact of floor-cleaning and furniture legs.

Stella McCartney UK flagship store, interior view (right)

Location: London, UK

Date: 2002

Designer: Universal Design Studio

The 'original' features such as skirting boards and cornices, which characterise this interior, were originally designed to conceal the meeting of floors and walls, and walls and ceilings, and the decorative fireplace continues to provide a focal point to the space. *Photograph by Richard Davies, provided courtesy of Universal Design Studio*

understanding the interior

the fundamentals of interior architecture
MATERIALS/texture

introduced elements

The extent of any intervention with the existing fabric will depend on the needs and strategies of the individual project. Where major spatial remodelling is called for, the introduction of new wall, floor and ceiling elements and their conjunction with the old, will require careful thought: not only in detailing of the junction between them but in the materials chosen to form the elements and make that junction. This is not just a matter of finding a construction method to do a job, but of architectural expression. Where old meets new, what respect or mastery is due to one or the other and how is that expressed?

Where the original meets the new there are fundamentally two strategies available to the designer. The first is to continue the new in the form of the old using the same materials and techniques. This approach tends to create **pastiche**, avoids the underlying expressive issues and is rarely entirely successful. The second is to create contrast in materials and forms so that old and new are identifiably, and honestly, different. In this second case the junction may be expressed in one of three ways:

- By (apparently) inserting the new into the old.
- By allowing the new to (apparently) hover clear of the old.
- By butting the new against the old.

The first two options are easily achieved by the creation of a gap that accentuates and celebrates the difference between the two elements. This **shadow gap** is an invaluable architectural device in such circumstances: a narrow gap, which visually separates two components while allowing structural connections to be hidden in the darkness of the created shadow. The third option is difficult to achieve convincingly even when differences of material make it expressively viable; not least because the surfaces in old buildings are rarely true or flat.

In addition to structural forms, building remodelling will include furniture and furnishings, the latter including floor and window coverings. In addition there are those things which, while strictly not part of the building fabric itself, need to be housed within or related to it: such things as light fittings and controls, ventilation and heating systems and, in some situations, audio components. Because of their fundamental independence from the building fabric, these elements may be regarded as transient artefacts that are able to respond to change and fashion more readily than the primary elements.

pastiche
An imitation of the work of a previous or similar artist, technique or period.

shadow gap
An architectural device that creates definition between two elements and, by creating a shadow, hides structural connections and discrepancies of finish.

London Loft, view through staircase void (left)

Location: London, UK

Date: 2004

Designer: Jonathan Stickland

The function of this staircase is more than just a means of connecting different levels – its sculptural form also provides a vista from above to below. *Photograph by James Morris <www.jamesmorris.info>, provided courtesy of Jonathan Stickland*

understanding the interior

Herzog & de Meuron (Switzerland)

1978

Notable projects:

Tate Modern, London, UK

Küppersmühle Museum of Modern Art, Duisburg, Germany

Jacques Herzog and Pierre de Meuron were both born in Basel in 1950, founding the Herzog & de Meuron Architecture Studio in Basel in 1978. They came to prominence with the conversion of Bankside Power Station in London to Tate Modern in 1995. They are well known for their experimentation with surface and material treatment and techniques and their ability to reveal unknown or unfamiliar relationships in architecture. Their work won them the Pritzker Prize in 2001 and is well known throughout Europe, Asia and America. In their remodelling of the Bankside Power Station for the Tate Modern, Herzog & de Meuron transformed the 3,400 square metres of floorspace in the Turbine Hall into a space that displays specially-commissioned work by contemporary artists.

Crafts Council 'Approaching Content' exhibition, view of book display (facing page)

Location: London, UK

Date: 2003

Designer: Nick Coombe

The mirrored plinth beneath the upright element within this display, gives the illusion that the whole structure seemingly defies the rules of gravity. Designers often attempt to deceive the eye in order to conceal structural detail, and to question our perception of our environment.

Photograph by David Churchill, provided courtesy of Nick Coombe

Crafts Council 'Contemporary Japanese Jewellery' exhibition display (below)

Location: London, UK

Date: 2001–02

Designer: Nick Coombe

This exhibition display appears to hover within the gallery space. It is part of the space yet, simultaneously, is only lightly connected to it.

Photograph by James Morris <www.jamesmorris.info>, provided courtesy of Nick Coombe

questions in summary
understanding the interior

1 2 3

How might the interior fabric of a building define the volumetric spaces within which the interior architect might work?

What constraints might the interior architect face when working with the integral elements of a space?

How might old elements be combined with the new?

45

Which elements
may be introduced
to the interior and
how might these
affect the volumetric
space?

What respect is due
to the old and the
new?

selecting materials

in this section

aesthetic qualities / performance specification / sustainability

Confronted with the need to specify materials and finishes for every aspect of the interior, the designer risks being overwhelmed by the breadth of choice available. The possibilities are literally limitless, both in terms of the materials and products themselves and of the manufacturers and suppliers offering variants of them. To take control of that choice, and to avoid being overwhelmed by it, it helps to identify the qualities required of any particular material by reference to four primary categories.

aesthetic qualities

In some ways this is the most difficult of the categories, simply because it is the one least susceptible to quantitative analysis. In making aesthetic decisions the designer will be endeavouring to give each surface and component its proper visual and tactile position in relation to every other surface and component. In order to get some traction on the huge range of possibilities available to the designer it helps to consider each element as having its place within a hierarchical sequence. Just as in every building there will be a hierarchy of spaces from the most important to the lowliest, so, within each space, a hierarchy of forms, surfaces and effects will serve to give identity and meaning to that space.

At the pinnacle of that spatial hierarchy will be the thing (or things) to which every other element of the space is subservient. This thing may not actually be part of the space itself: it could be a piece of furniture, an artwork or a view; but by recognising its importance (and its particular qualities and values) it becomes possible to make decisions about all the surfaces, materials and effects surrounding it and to ensure that nothing is done which will create visual chaos or ambiguity: something which designers strive to avoid.

Eliden, Lotte department store (above)

Location: Seoul, South Korea

Date: 2001

Designer: Universal Design Studio

The wall-finish to this retail environment subtly ornaments the space, and subverts the expectation that walls are inert building elements, which only play a functional role within an interior space. The surface treatment of this wall brings texture and complexity to the clothing and accessories on display.

Photograph by Yum Seunghuon, provided courtesy of Universal Design Studio

selecting materials

Barbican duplex refurbishment, view of kitchen (facing page)

Location: London, UK

Date: 2001

Designer: Nick Coombe

This domestic kitchen echoes the feel of its professional counterpart. The stainless steel worktop and 'handsfree' taps extend the metaphor here. This is a deliberately sterile space.

Photograph by David Churchill, provided courtesy of Nick Coombe

London Loft, view of kitchen (above)

Location: London, UK

Date: 2004

Designer: Jonathan Stickland

There are a number of finishes at play here. The white ceiling and walls are echoed in the worktop, and the dark timber floor finish is contrasted with a lighter timber veneer to the kitchen units and upstand beneath the island unit. It seems that the underneath and inside of different elements here are as important, if not more so, than those surfaces which are constantly on display. Note the rich pink inside to the cupboard on the right.

Photograph by James Morris <www.jamesmorris.info>, provided courtesy of Jonathan Stickland

Enric Miralles (Spain)

1955–2000

Notable projects:

Santa Caterina Market, Barcelona, Spain

The Catalan architect Enric Miralles studied architecture at the Barcelona School of Architecture, before graduating in 1978. His work is notably difficult to define, with heavy influences from Spanish architects as well as Le Corbusier and the Russian constructivist movement of the early twentieth century. Miralles's expressive designs can be seen to good effect in his native Barcelona – Santa Caterina market, Natural Gas Company tower and Diagonal Mar Park – but it is for the Scottish Parliament in Edinburgh that he is most widely known. Working with his wife and business partner Benedetta Tagliabue and the Scottish architects RMJM, he created an incredibly rich and diverse experience; as much landscape as design, with outstanding detail, material and spatial qualities. It won the Stirling Prize for Architecture in 2005. <www.mirallestagliabue.com>

selecting materials

MATERIALS/texture

performance specification

Every material and product available to the designer has individual performance characteristics, which encompass its strength and damage resistance, its workability and adaptability, its ability to accept surface finishes, its light reflectance and sound absorption and its capability of being fastened to other materials (and of accepting fastenings). Part of the designer's role is to understand these characteristics so that the appropriate product can be identified. Another part is to keep up to date with new and modified materials arriving in the marketplace.

The long-term maintenance implicit in the choice of materials is a performance issue that is easy to overlook, but is something that will have cost connotations for the client and which will have an effect on the way that the quality of the design is perceived over time. If the space is constructed of materials that are too fragile for their role it will quickly look shabby and unappealing, demanding an upkeep regime, which may be more onerous than the client is willing to fund. This may ultimately lead to ad-hoc on-site modifications, which will be to the detriment of the designed aesthetic. A large part of the designer's task is to predict the consequences of design decisions in relation to the activities and character of every space and to assess their viability in terms of their maintenance requirements.

Yoo Apartment, inside the snug (facing page)

Location: London, UK

Date: 2004

Designer: Blacksheep

The soft, cushioned surfaces of this environment create a sense of
intimacy and privacy. The materials used absorb sound from within,
and enable the space to remain 'hidden' from the rest of
the apartment.

Photograph by Gareth Gardner, provided courtesy of Blacksheep

**Tate and Centre Georges Pompidou exhibition,
'Abracadabra' (above)**

Location: London, UK

Date: 1999

Designer: Nick Coombe

The carpeted floor surface in this exhibition space absorbs sound
and engenders a sense of calm throughout. The dark colour of the
carpet further absorbs light adding to the 'designed' tranquillity of
the space.

*Photograph by James Morris <www.jamesmorris.info>, provided
courtesy of Nick Coombe*

selecting materials

MATERIALS/texture

sustainability

It has taken a long time to take effect, but there is a dawning recognition that we live on a planet with finite resources and an ecosytem that is not indestructible and that, although everything we do in life has an environmental impact, it is in our own interests to consider and reduce that impact as much as we can. Building work is particularly energy- and resource-hungry. As architectural designers we have a responsibility to take a whole-life view of the materials and products we use, taking into account the availability and extraction issues of raw materials, the environmental costs of transport and processing, their handling, fixing and maintenance regimes and, ultimately, their end-of-life dismantling and disposal.

Essentially the ideal is to use products and systems created and used at minimum environmental cost, which can be easily adapted and repurposed and which at the end of their working lives can be recycled or disposed of with minimum ecological impact. These principles are easy to define but hard to implement in the real world, as anyone who has watched skip loads of waste being removed from building sites will recognise. Unfortunately it is the real world, the one we rely on for our survival, which suffers when we fail to come to grips with these concerns.

cost

Although last on the list, the reality of any building project is that cost is a significant determinant of the material palette. Unless the chosen materials and their installation costs are affordable within the available budget there is little point in expending design time and energy on inappropriate and unaffordable choices. Having said that, it is also true that any design is a balancing act in which expensive choices in some areas may be counterbalanced by savings in others. Furthermore, in the dialogue between designer and client it might be possible to justify better quality materials on the basis that the more expensive material will offer savings in labour or long-term maintenance.

Burberry Millan flagship store (left)

Location: Milan, Italy

Date: 2002

Designer: Virgile and Stone

Retail environments tend to be relatively short-lived. Operating within the realms of high fashion, they are not usually designed for longevity. Nevertheless, despite the ephemerality of such spaces, the materials used in the interior are expensive and immaculately finished. Note in particular the timber parquet floor (re-used in part), the umbrella display and the high gloss sliding panels. The quality of materials and finishes used here reflect the identity of Burberry as a brand. Reconciling good quality design with the ephemerality of the fashion industry is an ongoing concern for the interior architect.

Photograph by Matteo Piazza, provided courtesy of Virgile and Stone

questions in summary
selecting materials

1

How can the interior architect take control of the chaos created by the myriad decisions to be made when selecting materials?

2 3 4

Should the interior architect be constrained by performance of various materials?

What role should sustainability play in the choice of materials?

Does cost reflect the perceived value of a material?

perception of quality

in this section

surface qualities / durability / connections

The possibilities for the construction and decoration of interior spaces include an extraordinarily diverse range of materials, finishes and products. By recognising the way that we respond to these things we are able to employ that response in the design of interiors. Of course, in modern interior architecture the international dimension to these issues means that the designer needs an awareness of both local and global cultural perceptions and traditions.

surface qualities

Recognition of materials generates perceptual understanding in the building user, but in the majority of situations it is not the structure of the material but its surface character that is important. This importance is partly to do with the material's perceived value (its connotations of affluence or cheapness, modernity or tradition) but also the way it responds to light and sound, and as a tactile experience. The last of these experiences, sometimes referred to as 'haptic' response, is a key component in our reaction not just to architecture but also to things found in nature, to products and to foods. We are all aware of surfaces and forms that demand to be touched, and which reward that touch, while others repel us. For many products the haptic values are an integral part of the brand. Bentley and Audi are marques for whom surface qualities are as important as the underlying engineering and which, in terms of fit, finish and conjunction of materials provide values that can be aspired to in architecture. It is often the case that the quality serves as no more than a signal of potential delight; but it is important that where materials invite touch they are detailed in ways that do not disappoint, are easily maintained and sustain those qualities over the long term by being resistant to marking and damage.

thomascook.com, office fit-out, internal view (left)

Location: Peterborough, UK

Date: 2001

Designer: Bluebottle

The entrance, which frames the view into the workplace, is constructed of gabions, which use a metal cage to house the stone fragments. There is a clear contrast between natural and machined materials here.

Photograph by Nathan Willock, provided courtesy of Bluebottle

durability

Some materials develop an appealing patina with age, others simply look tired and scruffy. The difference between 'natural' and 'man-made' qualities makes itself apparent in the way that materials age and in our response to that ageing. It seems we are more tolerant of wear in (apparently) natural materials than manufactured ones. The delight of manufactured surfaces is in their machine-age perfection. Unfortunately they are often easily marred by scratching and discolouration, at which point they lose that delight. Conversely, 'natural' materials such as timber and leather are in a constant state of change, but never lose their appeal. This must be, in part, recognition that quality relies on strength in depth and is not simply a superficial attribute. This recognition lies behind our reaction to surface coatings, which may be very appealing in their pristine state but which, because that appeal is literally microns deep, are susceptible to damage and need ongoing maintenance care. Surface coatings are traditionally extensively used in interior architecture: indeed, when thinking of 'interior design', it is often paint and wallpaper that first come to mind as representing that discipline. These coatings have many advantages: they are widely available in a huge variety of colours, patterns and textures; are easily applied; may be used to give a consistent skin to dissimilar surfaces and are readily changed and updated. The downside is that they are, by their nature, fragile and thus susceptible to wear and tear (and only too evidently create their own

record of that degradation). There is no escaping these disadvantages, but the designer will recognise them and take them into account in detail design. In particular it is at edges and corners that surface coatings are most vulnerable – partly because it is in these positions that they are most susceptible to physical damage. Many traditional details have their origins in a desire to take account of these susceptibilities. Dado rails and panels were designed to separate the wearing areas of walls from the cosmetic area above them; skirting boards were designed to resist the scuffing and damp of floor cleaning as much as to mask the junction between wall and floor. Victorian hospitals were designed using physically tough, easily cleaned materials to resist the damage caused by trolleys and beds, and to ensure hygiene. There is absolutely no necessity to maintain the forms and materials of these traditional details, but it is important that the designer recognises the issues involved and finds a modern and appropriate manner to resolve them.

Burberry Milan flagship store, window display (facing page)

Location: Milan, Italy

Date: 2002

Designer: Virgile and Stone

This window display for Burberry is an inside space pretending to be an outside environment. The materials used on the ground add to this illusion. The cobbled floor finish criss-crossed with the 'fake' grass strips, in conjunction with the timber 'sculpture' behind the dummies engenders this display area with a sense of the outdoors – the particular environment for which Burberry itself designs. *Photograph by Chris Gascoigne, provided courtesy of Virgile and Stone*

Tite Street, study (facing page)

Location: London, UK

Date: 2006

Designer: Blacksheep

The decorative wallpaper used in this study creates a focal point within the room, and adds depth and interest to the wall itself.

Photograph by Tony Murray, provided courtesy of Blacksheep

Burberry Milan flagship store, interior view (above)

Location: Milan, Italy

Date: 2002

Designer: Virgile and Stone

The slate floor, glass/resin plinths, steel staircase and glazed balustrading in the above retail space create a hard-edged environment that is softened through colour, light and the products on display. Such materials, rather than absorbing sound, tend to reflect it creating a reverberation of sound throughout the space. In this way, the designer can use materials and finishes to choreograph sound in space.

Photograph by Matteo Paizza, provided courtesy of Virgile and Stone

perception of quality

connections

It is not just the materials themselves that are important but the way in which they relate and are fastened to one another that determine the visual character of a space or thing. We would not be surprised to see exposed fastenings on natural materials (although we would consider the artefact more refined if those fastenings were nearly invisible), but would be shocked if our new MP3 players were nailed together. Once again it is a matter of context. The choice of fastenings, their position and spacing, make an important contribution to the narrative of the design. Modern structural adhesives and fixing systems make it possible to assemble many materials in a seamless and invisible manner, but, as individuals, we may find this slightly disconcerting: we seem to find comfort in being able to perceive how one element is fastened to another, particularly if those elements are of dissimilar materials. Different methods of fastening evoke different responses. Invisible fastenings suggest slickness but, at the same time, may imply inflexibility and inbuilt obsolescence. If we are unable to see how elements are attached we may marvel at their seamless perfection but may be uncomfortably aware that in a real world environment of change and damage we may be unable to replicate that perfection. Visible fastenings offer the reassurance of accessibility but need to be integrated and positioned in a way that complements rather than mars the material and form.

Of the visible fixings, engineered fastenings – particularly if hexagon or pin-drive headed – suggest a high-tech rigour; Pozidriv screws a low-tech pragmatism; dowels or timber-capped fixings suggest a traditional cabinet-making approach. These are rather simplistic approximations that will be modified by an awareness of the materials being joined, by the placing and rhythm of the fixings and by the degree to which they are visible, but which give a clue as to their importance as contributors to the designed aesthetic.

London Loft, interior view (above)

Location: London, UK

Date: 2004

Designer: Jonathan Stickland

The stone-finished storage unit, which extends across the wall above, conceals and then reveals its contents. When closed the floor and wall unit seem to fold into one another, and when open an abstract composition is created using the flat-screen TV and fireplace in contrast with the neutral tones of the material.
Photograph by James Morris <www.jamesmorris.info>, provided courtesy of Jonathan Stickland

Space NK, Spa NK view of reception (above)

Location: London, UK

Date: 2000

Designer: Virgile and Stone

This reception for Space NK consists of pure rectilinear forms, which are echoed in the straight lines of the cupboards behind the desk and in the timber floor panels. There are no skirting boards or edge details to conceal the junction between surfaces here – a difficult design to achieve.

Photograph by Chris Gascoigne, provided courtesy of Virgile and Stone

Allianz Arena VIP Lounge, interior view (right)

Location: Munich, Germany

Date: 2004

Designer: Virgile and Stone

The floor, walls and ceiling of this space appear to be a continuation of each other. The high-gloss finish to the large, sliding panels, are subtly different from the other 'white' surfaces in the space.

Photograph by Daniel Hildman and Andreas Grass, provided courtesy Virgile and Stone

perception of quality

questions in summary
perception of quality

1 2

How do we perceive quality in materials?

How do we respond to the visible finish of, feel of and connection between surfaces?

3 4

How do materials age and what will this mean for the interior architect?

How can the interior architect create connections between the new and the old in interior space?

perception of quality

architectural materials

in this section

timber / stone, slate & marble / concrete & terrazzo / metals / glass / plastics / leather & textiles

In the earlier sections of this chapter we have talked about the range of materials, and range of characteristics, available to the interior architect. In the following section we will identify some of the most commonly used materials, both natural and man-made, and identify the aesthetic and sensual qualities they can contribute to interior space.

Scottish Spa, general view (left)
Location: Isle of Islay, UK
Date: 2006
Designer: Jonathan Stickland
The major structural components of wall and roof are assembled using traditional vernacular methods. Note however, the way that the modernist white wall plane and the glass-block windows are defined as separate, almost independent elements.
Photograph courtesy of Jonathan Stickland

timber

Hugely versatile, timber may be employed structurally, as a surface cladding for walls, floors and ceilings and for many artefacts in the interior. Warm and tactile, timber may lend an elemental quality to a minimalist interior or be used to create the cosy ambience of a country retreat. As a renewable resource, timber has the potential to be an ecologically sound choice so long as its origin is documented and care taken to avoid supplies from unsustainable sources.

Left untreated, timber will absorb dirt and be susceptible to staining. Oils, varnishes, lacquers, waxes and paints may be used to protect the material. All will alter the surface appearance to a greater or lesser extent.

The principal timbers and their uses can be seen in the table below:

Ash	Pale, cream/white with an irregular striated pattern.	Floors, furniture.
Beech	Light pinkish brown with a straight grain.	Floors, furniture, worktops.
Birch	White/brown with regular striations.	Furniture, plywood.
Cedar	Rich red, weathering to silver grey.	Basins, tubs, furniture.
Cherry	Pinkish with a highly figured grain.	Flooring, furniture.
Elm	Light-brown with straight grain.	Interior joinery.
Maple	Cream, biscuit-brown with irregular grain.	Flooring.
Oak	Golden-brown with a tight, wavy, grain.	Furniture, joinery, flooring.
Pine	Yellow with prominent grain.	Flooring, furniture, construction.

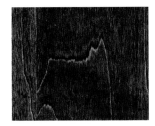

architectural materials

MATERIALS/texture

stone, slate & marble

Stone has been used as a building material for thousands of years and therefore has acquired connotations of permanence, tradition and solidity. A hard and heavy material, it tends to create noisy environments unless balanced by sound-absorbing materials. Modern quarrying and cutting techniques make it possible to create very large thin slabs of stone, which may be used for flooring or as a wall-cladding material. A natural and eminently reusable resource, the energy used in its transportation is of environmental concern.

The appearance of stone, slate and marble will depend on the particular rock formations in which they are found and on the extent to which they are finished and jointed. Rough, hewn stone with obvious joints will evoke a sense of rusticity, polished stone with hairline joints a more urbane aesthetic.

Hard, high-density stones such as granite are highly resistant to wear and staining, but the softer stones, limestone and sandstone, are porous and require careful sealing and maintenance.

 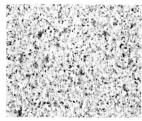 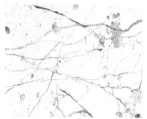 

Granite	Many shades from pink to black.	Worktops, flooring.
Limestone/ Sandstone	Shades of gold, pink, green and blue.	Flooring, bath surrounds, wall cladding.
Marble	A variety of colours and figurings.	Flooring, worktop inserts, wall cladding, baths and basins.
Slate	Blue-black to green-grey.	Steps, flooring, wall cladding.

concrete & terrazzo

Used by the Assyrians, Egyptians and Romans it was not until the early 1900s that the use of concrete became widespread in civil engineering projects. In the late twentieth century its extensive use as a material synonymous with brutalism created a reaction against its use. It has been rehabilitated in the past fifteen years as an honest, unpretentious material with industrial resonances. Because it is a semi-liquid material prior to hardening it can be mould-formed, taking on the texture and finish of that mould. An amalgam of water, cement and aggregate, the colour and texture of the finished material is dependent on the size and colour of the stone used for the aggregate. Additional colour may be introduced by adding pigment to the mix.

The appearance of concrete is dependent not just on the aggregate used and the way it is moulded but on its subsequent treatment. Pressure washing at the partly-cured stage will accentuate the aggregate. It can be wax polished to create a sleek satiny finish or treated with resin to create a wet-look gloss.

Terrazzo is a refined concrete, traditionally using marble chips as the aggregate, with the surface ground flat and polished after curing. This produces a very hardwearing material, which may be employed as flooring or moulded to create basins and splashbacks.

 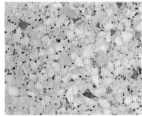 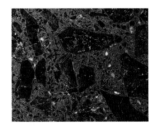 

Concrete	Grey to black.	Flooring, stairs, structural fabric.
Marble terrazzo	A variety of colours and figurings.	Flooring, countertops, bathroom units, splashbacks.
Granite terrazzo	A variety of colours and figurings.	Flooring, countertops, bathroom units, splashbacks.

architectural materials

MATERIALS/texture

metals

The use of metals as structural and industrial materials provides appropriate resonances for their use in contemporary interior architecture. Hard and unforgiving as surfaces, their planar, machine-aesthetic appearance can create a pleasing contrast with other, perhaps more organic, materials.

Most metals change appearance with oxidation, although in the interior environment this may happen imperceptibly slowly. Oxidation can be avoided by the use of surface lacquers or by polishing.

Metals are available in sheet form (flat, embossed or perforated) or as woven mesh as well as structural sections.

Aluminium	Silver-grey weathering to matt grey; anodising introduces colour and hardens the surface.	A soft metal that is usually found alloyed with other metals to give increased hardness. Window frames, cladding panels, floor covering, artefacts.
Copper	Reddish-orange.	Cladding panels, decorative features.
Mild steel	Silver-grey oxidising to red.	A tough, lightweight framing material. Oxidises easily and needs protecting by chroming, zinc plating, lacquer or powder coating.
Stainless steel	Silver-grey – mirror or satin.	A very hard material that resists oxidation. Used for kitchen and bathroom appliances, flooring and cladding.
Zinc	Silver oxidising to silver-grey.	A soft metal that is easily formed into countertops, splashbacks and cladding panels.

glass

If there is one material that has surpassed all expectations in the course of the past twenty years, it must be glass. For centuries a fragile material that demanded careful handling and cautious application, in the twentieth century it became a tough material capable of being used in structural applications that were previously thought the province of much more mundane materials.

In the modern architectural environment it is used as a replacement for walls and roofs, as a stair tread, balustrade and flooring material and as a replacement for timber in doors, shelves and work surfaces.

Using sand, soda and potash together with heat, glass can be created for a variety of applications and a range of appearances.

Float glass	Glass floated on molten tin to give a perfect surface.	Windows, mirrors.
Laminated glass	Glass panes bonded together with intermediate layers. Inter-layers may be coloured or printed.	Applications where there might be a risk of injury from breakage, structural applications.
Coloured glass	Tinted by application of dyes.	Windows, display units, internal lighting effects.
Low emissivity glass	Metal oxide micro layer.	Reduces infrared transmission.
Toughened glass	Heat-tempered and cooled.	Safety glass for use in doors, windows and other safety-related applications. Shatters into small square elements.
Figure-rolled glass	Formed between patterned rollers.	Internal decorative glass.

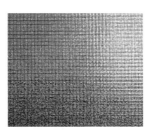
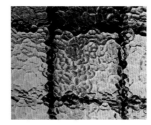

architectural materials

MATERIALS/texture

plastics

Plastics are ubiquitous in modern life: the principal materials in a range of artefacts found in the home, as leisure equipment and in industry. The first viable plastics were created in the second half of the nineteenth century. We would now regard those early plastics as being fragile and short-lived. Since then chemical engineering has produced a vast range of types and treatments that may be used as materials in their own right or as replacements for timber, glass, ceramics and metals.

Plastics may be moulded or extruded to make objects, films or fibres. In the last case the fibres may be woven or knitted to create textiles.

 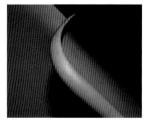  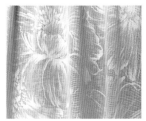

Acrylic	Usually created as a sheet material.	May be moulded to create furniture or used in sheet form as a tough, lightweight alternative to glass.
Corian	Trade name for a tough material of acrylic and natural minerals, which may be moulded and machined to shape.	Counter tops, display systems, bathroom and kitchen basins and sinks.
Melamine	Moulded or as a thin sheet.	Moulded as replacement for ceramics in bowls, cups and plates. As sheet material laminated to chipboard and other materials as a surface for worktops and furniture.
Polypropylene	A tough, versatile, mouldable material.	Furniture and household objects. As a translucent material it may be used as a light filter.
PVC	Cheap, lightweight, may be moulded or extruded.	Ubiquitous as flooring, windows, guttering, electrical insulation. Environmentally problematic.
Vinyl	May be moulded and printed.	Used as replica of natural products (timber, stone) in flooring and furniture.

leather & textiles

Leather and textiles are used in furniture and as wall and floor coverings to create a comfortable interface between the building structure and the human body. They may be employed to introduce contrast and a sensuous quality to the interior. Some fabrics are visually rich and warm to the touch, others cool and hard.

The choice of fabric will be determined by requirements of colour, texture and pattern and by the ability to withstand wear. They may be natural (from plants or animals) or man-made (from oil- or coal-based materials or modified forms of plant materials) or a blend of the two as a way of achieving a composite with qualities of each.

Leather/suede	Tanning process contributes a range of textures.	Upholstery, wall panels, floor covering.
Cotton	May be woven as a smooth or waffle fabric. May be glazed. May be woven with polyester fibres.	Soft furnishings, table and bed linen, window drapes. Cotton/polyester mixes produce a harder, less absorbent, fabric.
Linen	Takes dye well, may be woven to create a variety of textures.	Soft furnishings, table and bed linen, window drapes.
Silk	Takes dye well. May be woven to create a variety of textures.	Soft furnishings, wall panels, window drapes.
Velvet/velour	Woven (velvet) or knitted (velour) using silk, cotton or man-made materials.	A sensuous short-pile material used for soft furnishings, upholstery, window drapes.

questions in summary
architectural materials

1 2 3 4

What range of materials and finishes are available to the interior architect?

To what elements does timber lend itself well?

What sort of environment does stone and marble create?

How can the interior architect make use of concrete and terrazzo?

5 6 7 8

What sort of responses can metallic materials invoke?

For what elements might glass be suitable?

What range of plastics is available to the interior architect?

How can the choice of fabric create coloured, textured and patterned effects?

architectural materials

The designer can create the most eloquent space, crafted in exquisite detail using the finest materials in the most gorgeous colours, but, without light, he or she has wasted time, effort and money. Light and the effects of light are key to the enjoyment and functional success of spaces. The way that light impinges on the highpoints of surfaces, and the shadows created by its absence, allow us to perceive form and texture. It is light that allows us to discern differences in colour and tone. The painterly use of light, exemplified in the works of Johannes Vermeer, Ridley Scott and László Moholy-Nagy, can be employed by the architectural designer to create a mood appropriate to the particular brief, space and building.

understanding light

in this section

sunlight / daylight / responses to light / artificial light

Until man learnt to artificially replicate it, the fundamental source of light was the sun and in many respects sunlight remains the platonic ideal of light: its varying strength, colour values and direction bringing liveliness to the environment; changing through the day and from season to season.

sunlight

Sunlight is the word used to describe light from a visible sun; it is uni-directional and the light itself contains the full colour spectrum. This means that we see bright colours and sharp forms with crisp shadows. Sunlight has both a physiological and psychological effect on human beings. It follows from this that the well-being of the people using the spaces we design can be enhanced by introducing sunlight to the space (or at least offering the user the possibility of that light) and, where this is not feasible (for reasons of physical layout or seasonal shortage), replicating the character of sunlight by artificial means.

daylight

The term 'daylight' describes the light that is produced whenever the sun is above the horizon, but takes no account of whether it is actually visible. Thus it includes light produced in good conditions as direct sunlight as well as under poor conditions when it may be reflected and diffused by water vapour or atmospheric pollution. Under the latter conditions the light will be omni-directional and of a reduced spectrum, creating a perception of flatness of both form and colour.

Norman Foster (UK)

1935
Notable projects:
Great Court, British Museum, London, UK
Sackler Galleries, Royal Academy of Arts, London, UK
Canary Wharf Underground station, London, UK

Norman Foster is one of the most innovative architects of our time. Born in 1935, now Sir Norman Foster, he made his name as an architect of environmentally sensitive high-tech buildings and structures. He co-founded Team 4 with Richard Rogers before founding Foster Associates, which later became Foster + Partners – a high-profile company with an international body of work. His most famous projects include the remodelling of the Great Court at the British Museum and the new build of 30 St Mary Axe in central London.

**Besom Trust, existing site
(right)**
Location: London, UK
Date: 2005
Designer: Blacksheep
Note the saw-tooth roof profile
of this factory building, which
permits only reflected light into
the space.
*Photograph courtesy of
Blacksheep*

'Natural light is not flat. You feel the
day going and the clouds moving.
And then there's what I call a Magritte
moment. When daylight goes and you
start turning on the lights. Light makes
the room alive.'
Renzo Piano

responses to light

Our response to light is so complex that there can be no single ideal for places or people. We all have had experience of enjoying a cool, shaded space beyond the reach of a burning sun, admiring the play of light beyond the space, but comfortably distanced from it. Similarly we know how the same space in winter can seem chilly and uninviting unless we replicate the sun in the form of a fire. Our relationship with the sun is complicated by knowledge of the ways in which it can be damaging. The ultraviolet component of sunlight degrades plastics, bleaches fabrics and pictures and is damaging to human skin, so there are good reasons for controlling its incursion into buildings. It is further complicated by its constantly changing nature. One of the delights of natural light is the changes in direction, strength and colour that occur through the day and as a result of seasonal and weather patterns. This liveliness is not always welcome. There are undertakings for which changing light patterns may be a disadvantage or dangerous; curiously the obvious examples of this are at two extremes of human activity – art and manufacturing. For both these activities variations in the appearance of form with time are unacceptable and so both require windows orientated in such a way as to ensure that sunlight can never directly enter the space, but gain illumination indirectly by light reflected from the sky. Traditionally, in the northern hemisphere, artists' studios are illuminated by large north-facing windows while the iconic saw-tooth roof profile of factory buildings (known as 'monitor' roofs) are designed to permit only reflected light to enter the workspace.

Throughout history various methods have been employed to allow daylight to penetrate buildings. Early daylight openings were simply holes in the wall, devoid of glazing material and limited in size to keep out the weather. Thanks to the invention of glass, and its increasing availability and affordability, the potential size of the opening expanded so that, over time, it became possible to create buildings in which entire wall planes were made of glass. Not only has the size of the opening increased, but at the same time the support structures required by glazing have become reduced and refined to minimise their interruption of that opening. This trend has reached its current apogee in the use of glass as a structural material, employed both as glazing and framing. Between the primitive use of the hole-in-the-wall window and the Modernist invisible plane lie centuries of experimentation and creative endeavour as designers and architects pushed the boundaries of the available technologies. The results of some of these experiments are extraordinary. Hardwick Hall in Derbyshire, designed by Robert Smythson, is an Italianate Renaissance building in which the proportion of glazed area to solid wall is almost modernistic in its relationship, but which, to support its huge areas of glazing, uses traditional stone mullions and lead glazing cames in an amazingly delicate and refined way. The fact that Smythson was himself a master mason was probably the reason for his confidence in proposing and implementing this concept.

Stella McCartney US flagship store, window display (above)

Location: New York, USA

Date: 2002

Designer: Universal Design Studio

There are a number of reflective surfaces at play in this interior, which emphasise the urban context of this flagship store, and echo the city beyond.

Photograph by Frank Oudeman, provided courtesy of Universal Design Studio

LIGHT/mood

artificial light

It would be an unusual building, with unusual inhabitants, that was capable of functioning using natural light alone, and virtually all buildings with which interior architects work employ artificial illumination to replace or supplement natural light. Over the centuries tapers, candles and oil lamps have given way, first to gaslight, and ultimately to various forms of electric light. Each has had particular character, qualities and problems. In the design of the interior environment we are often endeavouring to replicate the positive aspects of systems and products while minimising or overcoming the shortcomings. This is as true of lighting systems as of any other. By identifying needs and developing a lighting design ethos that marries the requirements of space, activity and mood, it is possible to specify a lighting system that at one extreme may mimic the warmth and intimacy of candlelight and at the other provide the lighting levels and even distribution of a sports hall, with every conceivable variant in between. In fact, with sophisticated control systems, it is possible to create adjustable lighting that can modify the mood and capabilities of a space.

In practical terms artificial light is usually intended to do one of the following things:

- To provide the sole means of illumination at night.
- To augment the light provided by windows in order to provide better modelling.
- To provide light to compensate for poor natural lighting in winter or in poor weather conditions.
- To provide supplementary lighting where rooms are too deep for adequate natural lighting.

In addition to these tasks, electric light will be used for emergency and security purposes. We will not cover these last two issues in this book, but it is vital to integrate them in the design strategy in order that they do not appear as tacked-on afterthoughts.

Except in special situations where, for reasons of supply or effect, it would be an inappropriate choice, electric lighting is likely to be the norm. The range of

light sources and fittings is enormously extensive. For the designer the choice will be determined by the effect that needs to be achieved to meet aesthetic or practical goals, by the cost of the fitting and its power consumption and maintenance, and by the extent to which the light fitting itself contributes to the appearance of the space. On occasions it is desirable that the fitting is invisible. Although rays of light travel only in straight lines it is possible to use invisible light sources where the illumination is produced by bouncing the light off adjacent surfaces. This has the advantage of reducing the possibility of glare because, rather than a high-intensity light source, the eye sees a larger area of reduced luminosity.

Canteen, light detail (above)

Location: London, UK

Date: 2005

Designer: Universal Design Studio

The low-hanging pendant light above the table illuminates the dining experience.

Photograph by Simon Phipps, provided courtsey of Universal Design Studio

At the start of this chapter we identified two particular categories of lighting: task and background. The intention of the latter is that it should provide a general all-round level of light that will allow the building's users to navigate the space and to undertake non-critical tasks safely and comfortably. In appropriate circumstances background lighting may be augmented by accent lighting, which is used to highlight architectural features or objects. The luminous relationship between background and accent lighting will do much to determine the mood of the space – too great a disparity may appear unnecessarily dramatic, while background lighting that approaches the luminosity needed by accent lighting may make the space appear over-lit and brash. Task lighting is intended to give specific lighting conditions for localised functions – the application of make-up, reading or a manufacturing activity. The luminous relationship of background lighting to task lighting is vital in the creation of a comfortable visual environment. Too great a difference will lead to visual discomfort (think of watching television in a dark room) while too little will make it difficult to give the task the focus it warrants and will create an over-lit visual environment.

Schipol Airport, Central terminal, close-up (above)

Location: Airport, Central terminal

Date: 1997

Designer: Virgile and Stone

Artificial light is used in the above space to emphasise height – the space gets lighter the further up you look.
Photograph by Chris Gascoigne, provided courtesy of Virgile and Stone

Patek Philippe exhibition stand, view (left)

Location: Basel, Switzerland

Date: 1998

Designer: Virgile and Stone

The use of concealed lighting underneath the counter-top and skirting level suggests that each form is floating above the surface below.
Photograph by Ian McKinnel, provided courtesy of Virgile and Stone

LIGHT/mood

Radisson Hotel Domaquarée, view of staircase (above)

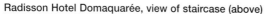

Location: Berlin, Germany

Date: 2002

Designer: Virgile and Stone

The staircase above has been very carefully lit to highlight each step and emphasise the direction of movement. The yellow/red glow at the top of the stair becomes a focal point to aim for.

Photograph by Chris Gascoigne, provided courtesy of Virgile and Stone

Radisson Hotel Domaquarée, lighting detail (above)

Location: Berlin, Germany

Date: 2002

Designer: Virgile and Stone

The illuminated 'icicles' not only create an interesting light sculpture, but their effect is multiplied by reflections from adjacent surfaces.

Photograph by Chris Gascoigne, provided courtesy of Virgile and Stone

**Hampstead House, kitchen
extension at night (left)**

Location: London, UK
Date: 2004
Designer: Blacksheep
A number of light fittings
combine to create the mood of
this space. The pendant light in
the kitchen generates a bright,
warm light, whilst the adjustable
light in the dining area
highlights the dining experience
itself. The wall lights articulate
the opening between the
two spaces.
*Photograph by Gareth
Gardner, provided courtesy
of Blacksheep*

questions in summary
understanding light

1 2 3

How do sunlight and daylight differ?

How do natural and man-made light differ?

How do humans react to light?

4 5 6 7

How can the interior architect make the most of available light?

How has light affected the design of buildings throughout history?

What is artificial light used for?

What is the difference between task and background lighting?

using light

in this section

light control / shadow & shade / colour

Despite the appeal of natural light, large, glazed elements are not always ideal or possible, as interior architects may well be constrained by the form and positioning of existing windows when remodelling an interior. However, it does help to understand the principles that will allow the designer to achieve the best results from daylight conditions.

windows

As a generalisation, in the northern hemisphere, south-facing windows maximise the potential for sunlight capture and for thermal gain: conversely, spaces with north-facing windows will receive only indirect natural light and will only ever lose heat. In the southern hemisphere the opposite is generally true. This loss of heat is to be deplored not just because of the loss of energy it represents but because, unless carefully designed double or triple glazing is employed, it may create condensation problems.

In practical terms this means that south-facing windows are usually to be preferred because of the psychological benefits of sunlight capture, but it also means that they will require some form of shading, particularly in the summer months, if the benefits are not to be outweighed by the discomfort of solar heat gain. Conversely, north-facing windows will never require solar shading but unless the process or activity within will be benefited by large amounts of indirect illumination (or the illuminated view beyond the window is spectacular) these are best minimised in size to reduce heat loss. A good example of the expression of these principles is provided by the Byker Wall in Newcastle (designed by Ralph Erskine): a one-kilometre ribbon of maisonettes that has extensive balconies and glazing on its south façade, but minimal window openings on the north face to reduce heat loss and to minimise noise intrusion from a proposed adjacent motorway.

The shape of the window, the depth of the wall in which it is housed and the colour and form of that housing all have an effect on the way that light enters the building, and the perception of that light by the building user. Tall, narrow windows allow light to penetrate deep into the building, producing illuminated swathes that move radially over the space as the sun tracks across the sky during the day, providing vertical snapshot views of the world outside. The horizontal ribbon windows beloved of Modernist architects create a formal separation of the living and ceiling planes, while providing a panoramic view of the landscape. With a ribbon window, the extent to which light is able to penetrate the space is entirely dependent on the position and height of the window in relation to the internal volume and planes.

The profile of the window surround and the window reveal, are as important as the size and shape of the glazing. Splayed reveals and reflective materials make best use of the available light and reduce the contrast between the light source and the unglazed part of the window wall. Right-angled reveals, particularly where the wall is thick and the window mounted towards the outside plane, limit the incursion of daylight and accentuate the contrast between the window wall and the window itself. This effect is further pronounced if the reveals are covered in a dark non-reflective material.

N1 Creative, studio area (right)

Location: London, UK

Date: 2002

Designer: Blacksheep

Creating exciting, yet usable workplace environments is a challenging task for any designer. The combination of a limited palette of colour and materials, and an open plan approach to the working space itself has generated a calm, friendly and democratic environment. The free-standing 'window' element contains the workspace, while framing the view to the city outside. This workplace is about making connections between public and private, company and employee.

Photograph by Louise Melchior, provided courtesy of Blacksheep

LIGHT/mood

light control

Internal blinds, curtains and shutters all have a role to play in controlling the light entering a space from the outside and help define the aesthetic identity and mood of the space. These light control devices can be created in an enormous range of types, styles, colours, textures and materials to suit the proposed identity of the space. By fitting such devices inside the window we simplify their operation but also deal with an issue to do with glazing, which is often unconsidered. We tend to think of window glass as a transparent (or sometimes translucent) medium. This is not always the case: sometimes it is a mirror. It is transparent only so long as the light is balanced inside and out, or in situations when the observer is on the darker side observing an illuminated scene beyond the glass. When the situation is reversed, the scene outside being dark and that inside illuminated, the glass mirrors the interior scene, making the exterior invisible.

This effect means that, if merchandise displays are going to be visible at night, shop windows need to be illuminated internally at least as brightly as the light on the pavement side, but in offices and domestic buildings, this also leads to the disconcerting realisation that the inhabitants of the space are on show to invisible observers outside. So curtains and

World Design and Trade Headquarters, general view (above)

Location: London, UK

Date: 2001

Designer: Universal Design Studio

Light is diffused through the screening below creating a calm, ambient light within the space. This effect is achieved by placing fluorescent tubes behind a layer of fibreglass with a polycarbonate sheet over the top.

Photograph by Dan Holdsworth, provided courtesy of Universal Design Studio

Radisson Hotel Domaquarée, view of atrium at night (above)

Location: Berlin, Germany

Date: 2002

Designer: Virgile and Stone

The glass in these façades is acting as a window into the space behind and, simultaneously, as a mirror of the streetscape.

Photograph by Chris Gascoigne, provided courtesy of Virgile and Stone

blinds hide the mirror effect, creating privacy for the building occupants. They also create a warmer environment, both visually and, by trapping heat, thermally. Where internal light control devices are less successful is in preventing solar gain. Once the sun's rays hit the glass, the greenhouse effect ensures a heat build-up on the inner side. Coatings applied to the glass at the manufacturing stage can modify this effect, but the most successful ploy is to stop the sun's rays hitting the glass in the first place. Traditionally this is achieved in hot countries by the use of external shutters and in modern buildings by the '*bris soleil*' which, extending horizontally at the top of the window, presents a series of louvres (sometimes adjustable), which act as a baffle to the sun at its zenith but allow the light to enter when the sun is lower in the sky in the evening and in winter. Carefully positioned planting may achieve the same effect. The use of deciduous planting ensures that leaf cover provides maximum shade in the summer months, while the bare branches in winter provide least obstruction to the weaker sunlight.

Volkswagen Autostadt , VW Collection (above)

Location: Wolfsburg, Germany

Date: 2000

Designer: Virgile and Stone

The objects in this interior are lit from above and below.

Photograph by Ian McKinnel, provided courtesy of Virgile and Stone

Radisson Hotel Domaquarée, view of bar (above)

Location: Berlin, Germany

Date: 2002

Designer: Virgile and Stone

The cool lighting below washes the back wall with light.

Photograph by Chris Gascoigne, provided courtesy of Virgile and Stone

using light

shadow & shade

So far in this chapter we have been concerned primarily with light, both natural and artificial. But architecturally it is often the absence of light that gives a real sense of three-dimensional form and adds character to spaces. The sunlit branches and leaves of the tree are made more dramatic by the shadow patterns cast on the trunk and the dark umbrella of the underside of the canopy. In a spatial context the glorious exterior vista is made more so by being perceived through an opening set in an under-lit wall and spaces generally appear richer and more enticing if areas of light contrast with pools of shadow. In a book regarded as a seminal work, *In Praise of Shadows*, Junichiro Tanizaki describes and investigates the value of shadow to the meaning and understanding of space and to the human psyche in the context of Japanese architecture and art – a book well worth exploring for an insight into this almost mystical subject.

Crafts Council Exhibition, 'Beauty and the Beast: New Swedish Design', detail of display in 'Beauty' gallery (below)

Location: London and Manchester, UK

Date: 2004–05

Designer: Nick Coombe

It is the plinths rather than the objects that are lit in this exhibition. This flattens the shadows yet emphasises the objects' form. Note that the backlighting is reflected off a three-metre reflective film to give an impression of *Aurora Borealis*.
Photograph by James Morris <www.jamesmorris.info>, provided courtesy of Nick Coombe

Allianz Arena VIP Lounge, internal view (left)

Location: Munich, Germany

Date: 2004

Designer: Virgile and Stone

Concealed lighting washes this space with delicate colour.

Photograph by Daniel Hildman and Andreas Grass, provided courtesy of Virgile and Stone

colour

The colour quality and strength of light sources, be they natural or artificial, have a considerable effect on the way we perceive colours. Colour is a contentious issue in interior architecture, not least because it is personal to us and is seen in relation not only to our individual ability to perceive it (and there is no easy way of being sure that others see colours in the same way that we do), but is heavily weighted by the values and resonance particular to us and to current fashion.

The colour wheel, relating the primary colours – red, yellow, blue – to one another and to their secondary and tertiary colours, is a useful graphic explanation of colour mixing and a convenient way of identifying complementary colours (colours opposite one another on the wheel) and harmonious colours (colours adjacent on the wheel), but the individual's response to these colours and their **tints**, **tones** and **shades** is problematic. Whether **colour psychology** properly describes the individual's reaction to applied colour in the contextualised environment is uncertain. An example will demonstrate the difficulty. Light green is often described as a calming and healing colour and, for that reason it has, since Victorian times, been widely adopted for hospitals and clinics. The question arises as to the point at which the reaction accorded to the colour in an abstract situation is overwhelmed by the response created by recognition of its usage – at an abstract level it is creating calm, at a contextualised level it may be creating tension. When we throw into the mix the issue of currency (is this a fashionable colour, and if so how is it used currently?), the simple response suggested by colour psychology may seem less assured.

In describing colour those at the red end of the spectrum are often referred to as 'warm' colours, those at the blue end 'cool'. Despite the difficulty of predicting the individual's response to a particular colour there are things that may be said about the relationship of colours one to another. Principal among these is that colours take on different qualities depending on their association (as an example, light grey seen on or adjacent to an area of black will appear white) and in relation to the direction, type and strength of the lights by which they are seen. Colours can appear radically different at different times of the day as daylight changes to direct sunlight, which in turn is succeeded by artificial light.

There is, of course, an international dimension to consider. Different cultures and religions ascribe different meanings to colour. In the United Kingdom red is the colour of urgency and potential danger; in Chinese societies it represents luck and happiness. What is without doubt is that the individual client will have a reaction to colour that will be probably expressed on a 'like' 'don't like' basis and that corporate clients will respond according to established brand values and identity. In a television interview Howard Hodgkin, that exemplary expressionist colourist, quoted David Hockney as saying 'It doesn't matter what colour you use'. It may well be that this is true not only of paintings but also interiors and that it is not the colours *per se* but the ways in which they are related one to another that is important.

---

tints
Adding white to the base colour produces a tint.

tones
Tones are the result of adding grey to the base colour.

shades
In colour terms the word shade is used to describe the result of adding black to the primary or secondary colours.

colour psychology
The study of mankind's sensory and emotional response to colour and its various forms.

Cuckoo Club, view into club (above)

Location: London, UK

Date: 2005

Designer: Blacksheep

The colour and materials used in this space are enhanced through the clever use of artificial light to create a sexy, intimate environment appropriate to the function of the space. Note the bar glittering in the background.

Photograph by Edmund Sumner, provided courtesy of Blacksheep

LIGHT/mood

**MBAM (Marble Bar Assets Management) trade floor,
reception area (right)**

Location: London, UK

Date: 2004

Designer: Blacksheep

Artificial light has been used in conjunction with strong/dark colour
here to create an intimate, atmospheric environment.

Photograph by Rob Howard, provided courtesy of Blacksheep

questions in summary
using light

1 2 3 4

| How can the interior architect make the most of the available light in an interior? | How does the orientation of a building affect the interior? | What role do windows play in the use of light in interiors? | How can the interior architect control the amount of light able to penetrate the interior? |

5 6 7 8

How can the interior architect control the side effects of lighting?	How does the function of an interior dictate the interior architect's ability to use light?	How can the interior architect use shadow and shade in the interior?	What effect can colour have on the mood and character of the interior?

calculating light

in this section

predicting daylight / calculating artificial light / glare

There is artistry to creating beautifully lit spaces, but it is an artistry that requires an understanding of the physics of light and the way that the human eye perceives and reacts to light.

predicting daylight

Because light is so important to our response to spaces it is vital that when presented with a commission to repurpose a building, we understand the quality and availability of daylight within the existing building envelope. These factors will be dependent on:

- The orientation of the building.
- The proportion of the space, or spaces, in relation to the size, position and form of the existing windows.
- The extent to which the building is overshadowed by surrounding buildings or trees.

This information can be gained in a number of ways. Firstly, a series of visits to the building under different conditions will give a series of, as it were, snapshots of light qualities at different times of the day and in different weathers. Because the eye is such an adaptable device, tolerant of a very wide range of light conditions, the use of a light meter will introduce some objectivity to the process. Although this method is a very effective way of getting a sense of the building in all its moods, it is unlikely that it will be possible to do this through the year, so a large degree of extrapolation will be needed. Secondly it is perfectly possible to get considerable insight by using a large-scale model, illuminated by a spotlight to represent the sun. Turning the model to represent the diurnal track of the sun and adjusting the spotlight to represent the effect of low-altitude sun in the morning and evening and throughout the day in winter gives a very immediate, if slightly crude, understanding of sunlight patterns and conditions. The same model placed outdoors on an overcast day will give an indication of light in unfavourable conditions. Finally, use of a computer model to analyse and predict lighting can provide a wealth of information for every required condition.

calculating artificial light

Earlier in this chapter we spoke of task, accent and background lighting. Of these, task lighting is the most critical in terms of light quantity and quality. The amount of light required to undertake a task will be dependent on the type of activity and on the individual undertaking it. The more intricate the task and the less the contrast between the components of that task, the greater the required light level will be.

The unit of light quantity is called the lumen and the light intensity required for tasks is usually described in lumens per square metre – lux for short. As an indication of the range of values required, a corridor or circulation space will require a minimum of 100 lux, 200–300 lux will be sufficient for dining areas while precision engineering or jewellery-making may require 1,500–2,000 lux. To put this in context an ordinary 100 watt domestic incandescent light bulb (properly called 'lamp') will produce in the order of 1,300 lumens.

Once the objectives of the lighting layout have been decided, the quantity of light required is identified from lighting tables. Light fittings may then be chosen to allow this level to be achieved, which are visually appropriate to the aesthetic of the space and control the shape and direction of the light pattern.

glare

If we accept that shadows are valuable, we nevertheless have to be mindful of problems created by extremes of contrast between light and shade, particularly when such contrasts are experienced in close proximity to one another. The human eye is an astonishingly adaptable device – able to function over a wide range of illumination levels from moonlight to brilliant sunshine. What it is unable to do is to accommodate both extremes simultaneously. In such situations glare may be created, giving rise to discomfort and, in extreme cases, vision disability. Some people are more susceptible than others to glare, but it is possible to reduce its likelihood by designing a controlled gradation of light between brightest and dimmest. Glare is most likely to occur when the light source itself (be that the sun or an artificial light) impinges on the field of view, which can be guarded against by considering viewing angles and by light control devices such as shades and louvres.

Daniel Libeskind (Germany)
1946
Notable projects:
Jewish Museum, Berlin, Germany
Imperial War Museum North, Manchester UK

Daniel Libeskind is well known for his deconstructivist discourse and is practised in the design of residential buildings, museums, hotels, public spaces and commercial environments all over the world. He was recently selected to design the structure to replace the World Trade Center towers in New York. His design of the Imperial War Museum in Manchester, UK, is based on the concept of a globe, shattered by the effects of war, and is furnished with iconic objects, such as artillery pieces and machinery. The floors are curved and the entrance tower is constructed of criss-crossing steel beams. Lighting is low level so as to add to the opressive atmosphere.
<www.daniel-libeskind.com>

calculating light

questions in summary
calculating light

1 2 3

How can the interior architect predict the effect that light will have on the interior and how can he or she use this to his or her full advantage?

What methods does the interior architect employ to predict natural light?

How can the interior architect calculate the various types of artificial light?

4 5

What problems can be caused by extremes of light and shade?

What devices can be employed to reduce discomfort caused by the extremes of light and shade?

Architectural design is a curious activity in that every building is its own prototype. Product, fashion, car and graphic designers expect to be able to create full-size models to test their ideas. But extraordinary though it may seem for an enterprise requiring huge expenditure of time, effort and money (and involving an army of specialists and contractors), the reality of building design is that the true qualities of the proposal are invisible until completion. To enable the architectural designer to deal with this issue, and to make the design proposal accessible to others, a variety of devices and methods have been developed with which to explore, test and communicate the design intentions of a project. This chapter describes methods used to present design information to the myriad of people requiring it during the course of the design and construction processes, and the techniques by which design qualities and ideas are represented.

key stages in design

in this section

the brief & design analysis / information gathering & design concept / design implementation /

project management & the building process

An architectural project progresses through four key stages in the transition from the client's first briefing to the handover of the finished building.

the brief & design analysis
In the early phase of this stage the client outlines the nature of the design task while, in turn, the designer explains the contribution that can be expected from the design process and the sequence of that process. This information will be formalised as the design brief and this will form part of the contractual agreement between client and designer in which fee structures, a description of the services to be provided and the stages of the project will be set out.

information gathering & design concept
A clear understanding of the building and its context is an essential prerequisite of design. In the course of this phase the parameters of the building (and its immediate surroundings) will be recorded as a building survey. Detailed information may be readily available for a new building, or one that has recently been modified, but the prudent designer will test this information for accuracy by checking overall and critical dimensions. At this stage the designer will want to make a photographic record of the existing building. Using the understanding of client need gained from the brief and design analysis, and the understanding of the existing building form and quality, the designer will develop a design concept. This concept will be communicated to the client as a design presentation. Agreement on the concept is necessary before the designer is able to embark on the next stage of the project.

thomascook.com, office fit-out, internal view (left)

Location: Peterborough, UK

Date: 2001

Designer: Bluebottle

A client's needs are articulated in the design brief. Thomas Cook, the client for this space, described their requirements to the designer who then interpreted them in built form.

Photograph by Nathan Willock, provided courtesy of Bluebottle

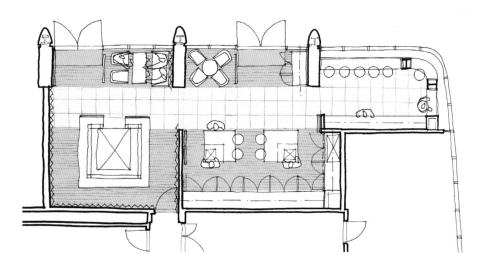

Citypoint Club (left)

Location: London, UK

Date: Ongoing

Designer: Blacksheep

A free-hand drawn plan is very useful for the initial stages of a project because it allows the designer to work through ideas and rapidly articulate their intentions.

Image courtesy of Blacksheep

key stages in design

design implementation

At this stage all the information required to transform the design proposal from concept to reality will be prepared and collated. This information will include working drawings and product specifications, which will be assembled as **tender documents** and presented to prospective builders and specialist contractors to enable them to supply **quotations**. At the same time the necessary **approvals** for the building works will be sought from local authorities. The contract for building work is generally created as an agreement between the client and the contractor (rather than between the designer and the contractor) so it is vital to keep the client informed and involved throughout this stage of the project.

project management & the building process

The designer may undertake the project management of the scheme or a professional project manager may handle this part of the process. Whoever is responsible has to ensure that a schedule of works and procurement schedules are created to identify the sequencing and timetabling of the various activities. On a project of any size a **planning supervisor** may be required. This stage will culminate in the formal handover of the completed building to the client.

tender documents

Documents setting out the extent and qualities of a project, provided to companies in order that they may quote prices and terms for undertaking the work.

quotations

A quotation is the offer by a supplier or contractor to undertake specified work to defined standards for a fixed price. It should not be confused with an estimate, which sets an approximate cost.

approvals

All building work is subject to rules and laws governing safety, amenity and integrity. Local authorities are responsible for ensuring compliance with these rules and laws, and their approval should be sought before embarking on changes. Changes to the use, size or appearance of the building require Planning Permission Approval. Structural, thermal, access, fire safety, drainage and hygiene standards are defined by the Building Regulations, and the designer is required to show that these standards have been met by applying for Building Regulation Approval.

planning supervisor

All commercial activity must accord with Health and Safety Regulations. Building sites are potentially dangerous places and the designer, contractors and personnel all have a responsibility for ensuring that the regulations are met. Commercial work that exceeds 30 man-days in work and/or more than 500 man-hours falls under Construction Design Management Regulations and will be overseen by a planning supervisor responsible for health and safety.

N1 Creative, existing site (left)

Location: London, UK

Date: 2004

Designer: Blacksheep

The site prior to the fit-out.

Photograph courtesy of Blacksheep

N1 Creative, office/meeting room (left)

Location: London, UK

Date: 2004

Designer: Blacksheep

Fit-out in progress.

Photograph courtesy of Blacksheep

N1 Creative (left)

Location: London, UK

Date: 2004

Designer: Blacksheep

Fit-out near completion.

Photograph courtesy of Blacksheep

key stages in design

questions in summary
key stages in design

1   2   3   4

What are the key stages of the interior architect's practice?

How does the interior architect use information taken from research and analysis of the existing building?

What information must be gathered by the interior architect and how will this inform the design?

How does the interior architect translate this knowledge into design?

5 6 7 8

How does the
interior architect
work with the client
throughout the
various stages of
the design process?

What issues must
the interior architect
be aware of when
formulating
proposals?

What role does the
interior architect
play in the actual
remodelling
process?

Who else will the
interior architect
need to work with
throughout the
design process?

representing design

in this section

sketching / drawings & visuals / orthographics / scale models / digital design

In addition to possessing excellent communication skills, the designer must be able to employ a range of skills to explore, develop and convey design ideas. Some of these are cheap and simple to employ, others require investment in materials and technology. The principal methods, devices and their application are explained here.

sketching

The simplest, cheapest and most versatile method of conveying ideas is by using pencil on paper. Despite the prevalence of computing in design, sketching retains a powerful appeal by dint of its immediacy and portability. In many circumstances being able to sketch quickly and accurately is an invaluable aid in the dialogue with others. Why struggle to describe an idea in words when it can be drawn? The ability to sketch is a valuable skill at initial stages of the design process and can also have a role to play on site as a way of explaining how problems of junctions and materials might be resolved. Although essentially throwaway products, sketches may also be scanned and transferred to the computer to be stored or developed further.

Hugh Grover Associates (facing page)

Location: London, UK

Date: 2006

Designer: Blacksheep

Concept sketches exploring design ideas.
Images courtesy of Blacksheep

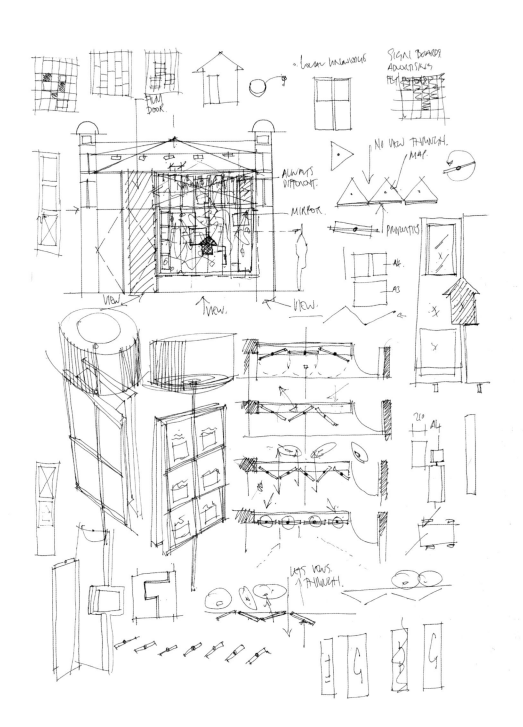

the fundamentals of interior architecture
PRESENTATION/representation

drawings & visuals

The difference between sketching and drawing is a subtle one, but principally is one of intention. Where a sketch is intended to show a preliminary idea or act as a device for identifying and outlining a particular aspect, a drawing is an altogether more complete and considered artefact and one that may make use of mechanical aids – drawing boards and drafting devices such as compasses and set squares – or a computer. Drawings are often utilised to generate a sense of three-dimensional spatial quality by employing the mechanics of perspective and by the application of colour and shading to suggest material and lighting qualities. At their most sophisticated these may be indistinguishable from photo reality. Drawings of this type are often referred to as visuals and are the principal means by which the designer explains concepts and final designs to the client.

Visuals may be manually generated by applying rules of perspective to a set of **orthographic drawings** at a drawing board or may be extracted from a **three-dimensional computer model**. The latter has the tremendous advantage of allowing speedy adjustment of viewpoint (the position adopted by a notional inhabitant of the space), angle of vision and focus point in order to achieve the most effective result. The downside is that, for a building of any complexity, the time taken to model it may be not insignificant. Many designers are able to create useful perspective views as free-hand drawings – these can be invaluable in the early stages of a project.

Colour may be incorporated in drawings by using artist or graphic media – colour wash, coloured pencil, letratone, pastels or markers – or by using proprietary computer software such as Photoshop to **render** and **texture-map** the image.

orthographic drawings

A set of drawing conventions in which any sense of perspective is eliminated, as if the building is viewed from an infinite distance.

three-dimensional computer model

A three-dimensional representation of geometric data, stored and generated by a computer.

rendering

Rendering software uses colour and lighting to represent the intended reality of a building using a computer model or image from a computer model. Depending on the quality of the software and computer, and the needs and proficiency of the user, it is possible to create images that are indistinguishable from reality.

texture mapping

Software that applies pattern and texture to the surfaces of a computer model in order to represent real life materials.

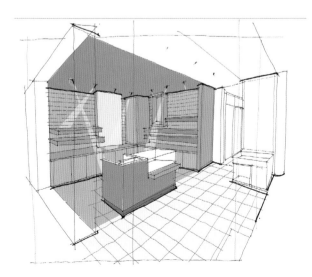

MBAM (Marble Bar Asset Management), trade floor (above)

Location: London, UK

Designer: Blacksheep

Date: 2004

An example of hand-drawn visualisation technique.

Images courtesy of Blacksheep

Citypoint Club (left)

Location: London, UK

Designer: Blacksheep

Date: Ongoing

A sketch presentation of the visualised design.

Images courtesy of Blacksheep

representing design

**Hugh Grover Associates,
store front (left)**

Location: London, UK

Date: 2006

Designer: Blacksheep

This is a sketch presentation visual to show the client. It is a deliberately informal drawing that suggests to the client that the design proposals are at a developmental stage.
Image courtesy of Blacksheep

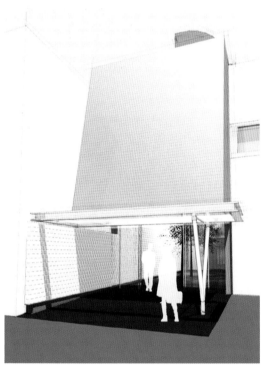

The Base, Virgin Atlantic Airways (left and below)

Location: Gatwick, UK

Date: 2007

Designer: Universal Design Studio

Computer images showing the entrance to the staff training centre.

Images courtesy of Universal Design Studio

representing design

the fundamentals of interior architecture
PRESENTATION/representation

orthographics

The word orthographic is used to describe a set of drawing conventions in which any sense of perspective is eliminated, as if the building is viewed from an infinite distance. These conventions are the basis of what are referred to as working drawings – the drawings that are required to get the work constructed. It will be appreciated that, other than offering a vision of the finished product, perspective drawings are useless as a means of informing builders and suppliers because they offer no dimensional information. Orthographic drawings, on the other hand, give little insight into the qualities of the finished building (although the experienced professional is able to 'read' these qualities from such drawings), but offer insight into the dimensional relationship between the parts and the whole. In order to do this orthographic drawings are made to scale: that is every line is drawn as a fixed proportion of the size of the real thing. The scale chosen will depend on the amount of information to be included and the degree of detail to be expressed; thus most interior layout drawings will be at 1:50 (in other words every part is drawn as one fiftieth of full-size), while intricate construction details might be drawn at 1:5, 1:2 or 1:1 (full size).

There are two principal types of orthographic drawings: **sections** and **elevations**. Sections are created by taking a slice through the building as if with a giant knife so that we are able to see the structure and construction at the cut line and the spaces beyond it. Where this slice is taken vertically through the building the result is referred to as a 'vertical section', or often simply the 'section'. Where the slice is taken horizontally the result is referred to as the 'plan section', or, more frequently, simply the 'plan'. There are few rules for the positioning of sections: their role is to convey information so that whatever does this most effectively will be correct. By convention plans are usually the result of sections created at around 1200–1500mm above floor level, but this may be modified by special needs and circumstances. If we were to look past the cut line of a vertical section our view of the space beyond it would usually be terminated by a wall; either an internal partition wall or the inside of an external wall. This wall would be described as an elevation because it is drawn as a flat plane without any perspective effect. The word elevation is also often used to describe the external façade of a building, again drawn without reference to any perspective effect (although the illusion of perspective depth is sometimes created by casting shadow patterns from protuberances on the wall by a process known as sciagraphy).

The plan and section are the standard design and working drawings, and from them a range of other drawings may be produced. The perspective visual relies on the relationship of parts developed in orthographic drawings as do the two most common forms of non-perspectival three-dimensional drawings: the **isometric** and **axonometric** projections. These projections were developed, probably from engineering drawing practice, as a means of conveying some sense of form and space while remaining scalable. They look slightly strange to those accustomed to perspective drawings, but do have their uses (they can be helpful in describing bathroom and kitchen layouts for instance) and are relatively quick to create.

sections

Section drawings are imagined 'slices' through a building or interior. They are useful as a means of assessing the relationship and proportions of spaces.

elevations

Elevation drawings display the façade of a building and are often used in conjunction with plans.

isometric

A three-dimensional drawing where the three principle dimensions are represented by three axes 120 degrees apart, with all measurements on the same scale.

axonometric

The simplest means of producing a three-dimensional view of the interior space. The plan of the interior is drawn at an angle of 45 degrees from the horizontal or vertical plane.

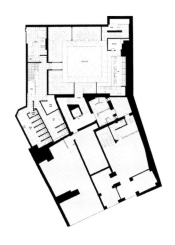

Cuckoo Club (left)

Location: London, UK

Date: 2005

Designer: Blacksheep

A plan drawn on the computer allows the designer to make necessary changes to working drawings with ease.

Images courtesy of Blacksheep

The Base, Virgin Atlantic Airways (below)

Location: Gatwick, UK

Date: 2007

Designer: Universal Design Studio

A vertical section through this scheme enables the designer to show the conical forms, which will funnel light to the space below.

Images courtesy of Universal Design Studio

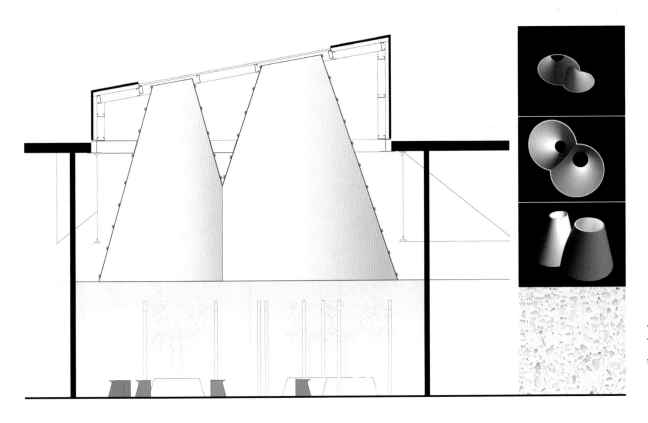

the fundamentals of interior architecture
PRESENTATION/representation

Voyage (below)

Location: London, UK

Date: 2003

Designer: Blacksheep

These hand-drawn axonometrics describe the designer's proposals for the ground floor and basement of a shop. Again these are not working drawings from which to build, but drawings that express design intentions.

Images courtesy of Blacksheep

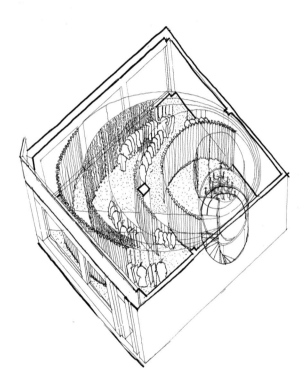
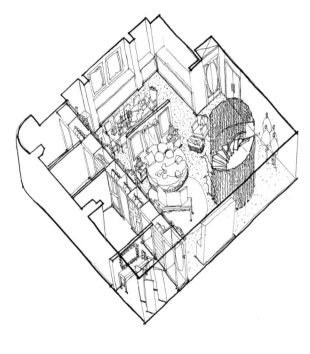

Ludwig Mies van der Rohe (Germany)

1886

Notable projects:

New National Gallery, Berlin, Germany

Born 1886 Ludwig Mies van der Rohe is acknowledged as one of the most influential architects of the twentieth century. Briefly director of the Bauhaus after architectural commissions in Germany and Holland, he emigrated to the United States in 1937 where he was responsible for many of the seminal works of modern architecture. Famous for coining the axiom 'less is more', Mies van der Rohe set out to create spaces that were based on material integrity and sound structural methods. His interiors are known for their calmness and are an inspiration to many interior architects today.

scale models

Since the intention of interior architecture is to create a spatial experience, the obvious way to represent this is to create it in miniature – a scale model. For those with the dexterity to make them there is no doubt models are an invaluable design tool for developing and understanding space and form. Furthermore, of all the promotional devices available to the designer they are the most easily understood by the non-designer. The real difficulty with creating a model is in knowing when to stop! The model is hugely useful in allowing the viewer to imagine his or herself inside the space but there comes a point where to replicate the amount of detail that would exist within a real interior makes the model seem toy-like and unreal. Colour too is problematic in models. Colour is not really a scalable entity, but somehow it has to be if it is not to appear overwhelming in a miniature space. These shortcomings mean that the most successful models are those that allude to spatial and material qualities rather than mimicking them. It is for this reason that architectural models are often made in white or muted colours in order to focus attention on the spatial and structural form, with coloured visuals used to augment this information.

Schipol Airport, Central terminal (above)

Location:	Amsterdam, The Netherlands
Date:	1997
Designer:	Virgile and Stone

Models are a very immediate way of communicating three-dimensional design ideas to others. They are much easier to 'read' than drawings, particularly orthographic drawings, which require specialist knowledge and experience to understand.
Image courtesy of Virgile and Stone

Student model (above)

Location:	Concept work only
Date:	Concept work only
Designer:	Concept work only

A student's model, lit and photographed, communicates the design potential of an idea immediately. Such images seduce the eye.
Image courtesy of Middlesex University

Hugh Grover Associates, store front (left and below)

Location: London, UK

Date: 2006

Designer: Blacksheep

A series of very simple models, lit and photographed, can successfully communicate a design concept without the need for a verbal commentary.

Images courtesy of Blacksheep

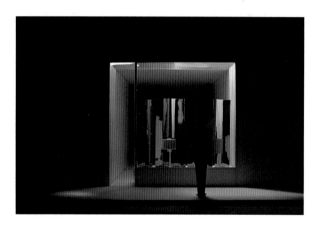

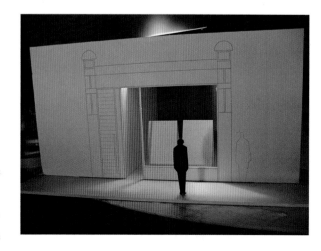

digital design

The digital revolution has ensured that the techniques and conventions that were once the province of the artist or draughtsman are now available via the computer. The great advantage of the computer to the professional designer is that it makes possible the cross-relation of every piece of project information; drawings, text and specifications in a single database. When properly managed this ensures that all information is consistent and up to date and, with appropriate safeguards, accessible to all who are involved on the project. From a project management standpoint this is a valuable attribute. The computer also makes skills and techniques that were once the province of specialists more accessible: the creation of visuals is the obvious example of an activity that, although time-consuming, has been made more accessible and cost-effective by the use of the computer. Part of the reason for this has been the development of 3D modelling techniques. Where once design drawings were initiated in two dimensions, being extended into three dimensions by the use of models and visuals, now it is feasible to build a three-dimensional computer model at the outset, abstracting two-dimensional drawings from this model. Not only is this a more appropriate sequence of working, it also allows the possibility of creating unlimited numbers of sections and visuals from the primary model – not because numbers are valuable *per se*, but because the ease of production makes it possible to explore and identify exactly the right drawing for each purpose.

Computer texture-mapping and rendering techniques allow the designer to experiment with colour, texture and lighting positions and effects, and to express these as colour visuals. The computing power and time required to create a visual of a complex spatial and lighting scheme may be considerable, but the final effect is one that is not easily achieved in any other way. Until recently the expression of three-dimensionality was only achievable as a series of two-dimensional visuals or as an on-screen walk-through of the space. However, recent developments in printing techniques make it possible to build a true three-dimensional model; building up a resin material in successive layers each only microns thick to create a scale facsimile of the building. As these techniques are developed and refined the designer will be able to spend more time working in three dimensions and less in two to the advantage of the design process.

Palmers Textil AG (right)
Location: Austria
Date: Concept work only
Designer: Universal Design Studio
This computer-generated visual creates an impression of the façade of the scheme. Its ethereal quality suggests that the design proposals are at a conceptual stage and yet to be firmed up.
Image courtesy of Universal Design Studio

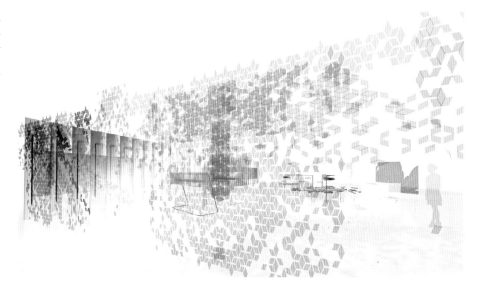

Bistroteque, bar and venue (above)

Location: Unknown

Date: 2004

Designer: Bluebottle

Photoshop visual of the proposed change of use and fit-out.

Image courtesy of Bluebottle

Voyage flagship store (above)

Location: London, UK

Date: 2003

Designer: Blacksheep

CAD visual of the entrance to the store.

Image courtesy of Blacksheep

questions in summary
representing design

1 2 3 4

| How can the interior architect best represent his or her ideas for the redesign? | What advantages and disadvantages do each representation technique have? | Which drawing technique is most suitable for the various stages of the design process? | How can the interior architect provide a sense of perspective, scale and proportion? |

5 6 7 8

What communication skills must the effective interior architect possess?

How can the interior architect use models to convey design ideas?

How effective are computer-generated visualisation techniques?

What are the advantages and disadvantages of computer-generated visuals?

conclusion

Interior architecture is a complex and deeply-layered activity, which is at the service of all human needs.

It is involved in the creation of appropriate environments to serve practical purposes but, just as importantly, it also caters for those less-easily defined aspects of human existence: the desire for emotional sustenance and for meaning.

This book has introduced the practical necessities of designing interior environments and of conveying the qualities of that design to the client who will finance it, and the contractors who will make it tangible; but more than that our intention has been to identify the emotional and sensual needs of the building user and introduce a way of considering and evaluating design issues.

Design is a way of life. This is particularly true for the interior architect for whom every journey offers examples of spatial forms and devices, effects of light and of material constructions; all of which may be mentally stored away for future recycling. One of the most valuable tools for the aspiring designer is an enquiring eye: we trust that the images in this book have inspired you to look further.

Our particular thanks are due to the practices and designers whose examples of work have done so much to demonstrate the excitement and value of interior architecture.

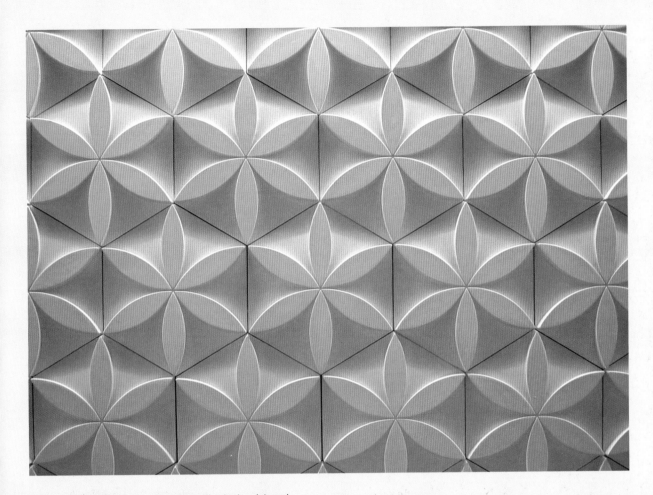

Stella McCartney US flagship store, tile design (above)

Location: New York, US

Date: 2002

Designer: Universal Design Studio

Having established the broad conceptual approach to a given project, designers will begin to focus in on specific junctions and details. The bespoke tile design for Stella McCartney New York would have been arrived at long after initial decisions had been made about the organisation, mood and material qualities of the space. Interior architects work at both ends of the design scale, establishing an overall spatial approach as well as defining the intimate relationship between different elements in that space. *Photograph by Frank Oudeman, provided courtesy of Universal Design Studio.*

conclusion

sources of information and inspiration

The following books, periodicals and artists will extend your understanding of the issues identified in this book and show how the principles may be extended and employed.

books

Brand, S. 1997. *How Buildings Learn*.
London: Phoenix

Brooker, G. & Stone, S. 2004. *Re-Readings: Interior Architecture and the Design Principles of Remodelling Existing Buildings*.
London: RIBA Enterprises

Lawson, B. 2003. *How Designers Think*.
Oxford: Architectural Press

Lawson, B. 2001. *The Language of Space*.
Oxford: Architectural Press

Massey, A. 1990. *Interior Design of the 20th Century*. London: Thames & Hudson

Melvin, J. 2005. *...Isms: Understanding Architecture*. London: Herbert Press

Papanek, V. 1985. *Design for the Real World*.
London: Thames & Hudson

Porter, T. & Goodman, S. 1992. *Design Drawing Techniques for Architects, Graphic Designers and Artists*.
London: Butterworth Architecture

Reid, E. 1997. *Understanding Buildings: A Multidisciplinary Approach*. Harlow: Longman

Salvadori, M. 2002. *Why Buildings Stand Up: The Strength of Architecture*. New York: WW Norton

de Sausmarez, M. 2002. *Basic Design: The Dynamics of Visual Form*. London: Herbert Press

Tanizaki, J. 2001. *In Praise of Shadows*.
London: Vintage Classics

Thiel-Siling, S. (ed.) 2005. *Icons of Architecture: The 20th Century*. London: Prestel Verlag

Wolfe, T. 1982. *From Bauhaus to Our House*.
London: Jonathan Cape

periodicals

Architectural Review
Domus
Frame
Wallpaper

artists

James Turrell
Andy Goldsworthy
Mary Miss
Howard Hodgkin

conclusion

The world is full of fascinating buildings. Within this book we have identified and illustrated the work of many important architects and designers, but, inevitably, these form only a minuscule proportion of the total.

We hope that we have provided an insight into the way that buildings work and the way that people respond to them, but the best way to understand building design is to experience it for yourself. The following buildings vary in scale and stature. Some are virtually national monuments, others are localised responses to particular sites and needs. Some are by internationally renowned architectural practices, others by smaller practices. All embody the principles that have been presented in this book.

Hill House, Helensburgh, UK.
Charles Rennie Mackintosh

Glasgow School of Art, Glasgow, UK.
Charles Rennie Mackintosh

Dundee Contemporary Arts, Dundee, UK.
Richard Murphy Architects

Scottish Parliament Building, Edinburgh, UK.
Enric Mirralles (EMBT with RMJM)

Scottish National Poetry Library, Edinburgh, UK.
Malcolm Fraser Architects

Welsh National Assembly, Cardiff, UK.
Richard Rogers Partnership

De La Warr Pavilion, Bexhill on Sea, Sussex, UK.
Mendelsohn and Chermayeff

Great Court, British Museum, London, UK.
Foster + Partners

Royal Festival Hall, Belvedere Road, London, UK.
Leslie Martin, Peter Moro & LCC

Hammersmith Health Centre, London, UK.
Guy Greenfield Architects

Laban Dance Centre, Deptford, London, UK.
Herzog & de Meuron

Pacific Palisades, Los Angeles, USA.
Charles and Ray Eames

Unity Temple, Oak Park, Chicago, USA.
Frank Lloyd Wright

Schröder-Schräder House, Utrecht, Netherlands.
Gerrit Rietveld

German Pavilion, Barcelona, Spain.
Mies van der Rohe

Villa Mairea, Noormarku, Finland.
Alvar Aalto

Ronchamp Chapel, Belfort, France.
Le Corbusier

Church of Light, Osaka, Japan.
Tadao Ando

Staatsgalerie Extension, Stuttgart, Germany.
James Stirling, Michael Wilford & Associates

index

Page numbers in *italics* denote illustrations.

A
Aalto, Alvar   80
accent lighting   125
accessibility   41
acoustics   60
        see also sound
Adaptive Reuse   18
aesthetic qualities, materials
                                88–91
airports   69
Allianz VIP stadium lounge
                                105, 135
analysis
design analysis   148
site analysis   46–57
anthropometrics   60
approvals   150
architectural materials   108–17
architraves   81
artificial light   124–7, *137–9*, 143
Autostadt   *133*
axonometric drawings   160, *162*

B
background lighting   125, *134*
Barbican apartments   *19, 90*, 91
Battersea Power Station   *17, 69*
Besom Trust site   *51, 121*
Bistroteque bar and venue   *166*
brand values   58, 60
the brief   148–9
bris soleil   133
British Red Cross headquarters
                                40, 41
building process   150
building reuse   10, 18–21
building typology   48
Burberry   store
            61, 94–5, 100, *101, 103*

C
calculating light   142–5
Canary Wharf Underground
station   *11*
Citypoint Club   *149, 157*
coatings   100
colour   49, 136–9, *163*
column-and-slab systems   50
composition   24–43
computer   models
            156–7, *159*, 165–7
concepts *see* design concept
concrete   111
connections   104–5
conscious deliberation   55, 64
construction   48
contextual framework   45
controlling light   132–3, 143

cost of materials   95
Crafts Council   *72–3, 84–5*, 134
Cuckoo Club   *10, 137, 161*

D
daylight   120, 122, 142
        see also light
de Meuron, Pierre   84
design analysis   148
design concepts   *10*, 70, 148
design implementation   150
design process
            47, 148–53, 168–9
dialogue   48
digital design   165–7
Disability Discrimination Act 1995
                                41
display   60–1, *72–3*, 100, *101*
doors   38
drainage pipes   55
drawings   26, 156–7, 160–1, *162*
        see also sketching
durability of materials   100

E
Eames, Charles and Ray   71
electric lighting   124
elements   24–43, 78–84
elevation drawings   160
Eliden, Lotte   *28–9, 89*
ergonomics   60
escalators   36
exhibitions
        72–3, 84–5, 93, 125, 134
externalisation of ideas   64

F
fabric of buildings   18, 78–81
fabrics *see* textiles
façades   18
fastenings   104
Fibonacci Sequence   30–1
form   14–43
Foster, Norman   120
frame systems   50
function   18, 44–75

G
gardens   32
genius loci   17
glare   143
glass   35–6, 49, 113, 122, 132
Golden Section   30–1
granite   110–11

H
Hadid, Zaha   34
Hampstead House *33–4, 80, 127*

Hanover Expo   *79*
haptic values   98
heat loss   130
Herzog, Jacques   84
hierarchy of spaces   88
history   16, 46–7, 78, 81
home offices   64
hospitals   71
hotel accommodation   66, 68
Hugh Grover Associates
            154, *155, 158, 164*

I
information gathering   148
integral elements   78–81
interior architects
definition   13
role   10, 16–17
interior architecture definition   9
interiors, types of   58–75
understanding   78–87
introduced elements   82–4
Irish pavilion, Hanover Expo   *79*
isometric drawings   160

J-K
Jacobsen, Arne   26
Koolhaas, Rem   70

L
Le Corbusier   30–1
leather   115
Libeskind, Daniel   143
lifts   36
light   49, *67*, 118–45
calculating   142–5
control   132–3, 143
responses to   122
understanding   120–9
using   130–41
living spaces   66–8
Lloyd Wright, Frank   36
loadbearing walls   50
London Loft *37, 54, 83, 91, 104*
Loos, Adolf   30
lumens/lux   143

M
maintenance of materials   92
marble   110–11
Marble Bar Asset Management
see MBAM
materials   76–117
MBAM trading floor
        12, 13, *39, 138–9, 157*
Meier, Richard   32, 36
metals   112
Miles van der Rohe, Ludwig   *162*

Millennium Dome 8, 9
Miralles, Enric 91
models 156–7, 159, 163–4, 165–7
The Modulor 30–1
mood 118–45
movement 34–6

N
N1 Creative 131, 151
natural light see light

O
openings 122, 127
 see also doors; windows
orientation 49
orthographic drawings 156, 160

P
Palmers Textil AG 165
pastiche 82
Patek Philippe exhibition stand 26, 125
Pembridge Villas 67
perception of quality 98–107
performance of materials 92–3
periodicals 172
Piano, Renzo 47
place 16–23
plane 24, 25
planning supervisors 150
plastics 114
Pompidou Centre exhibition 93
position 46, 49
post-and-beam structures 50
predicting daylight 142
presentation 146–69
preservation 18
project management 150
proportion 30–1
psychology 136
public spaces 69

Q
quality of materials 88–91, 98–107
quotations 150

R
Radisson SAS Hotel 126, 132–3
ramps 36
religious buildings 69
remodelling 18
rendering 156, 165
renovation 18
representation 146–69
responses to light 122
restoration 18

restorative spaces 70–1
retail spaces 58–61, 94–5
reuse of buildings 10, 18–21
ribbon windows 131
Rietveld, Gerrit 64

S
scale 26
scale models 163–4
Scarpa, Carlo 18
Schipol 125, 163
Scottish Spa 52–3, 108
section drawings 160–1
sense of place 16–17
sensory experiences 9, 77, 170
services 55
shade/shadow 134
shades of colour 136
shadow 134
shadow gaps 82
shell structures 52
site 44–75
sketching 154, 155, 157–8
 see also drawings
skirtings 81
slate 110
Smythson, Robert 122
sound 103
 see also acoustics
space 14–43, 88
Space NK 61, 70, 105
stairs 35–6, 37, 83, 126
Starck, Philippe 66, 68
Stella McCartney stores 20–1, 49, 59, 81, 123, 171
stone 110–11
structure 18, 50–3
sunlight 120, 122, 133, 142
 see also light
surface coatings 100
surface qualities, materials 98
sustainability 94

T
tabula rasa 16
task lighting 125, 143
Tate exhibition 93
tender documents 150
terrazzo 111
textiles 115
texture 76–117
texture mapping 156, 165
Thomas Cook Accoladia 25, 63
thomascook.com office 48, 65, 99, 149
three-dimensional models 156–7, 159, 165–7
timber 109

time constraints 68
tints 136
Tite Street study 102, 103
tones 136
transient spaces 72–3
transition 38, 39
typology 48

U
unconscious deliberation 55, 64

V
Villa Arena centre 27, 35
Virgin Atlantic Airways 159, 161
vista 32
visuals 156–8
Voyage stores 162, 167

W
walls 50, 55
windows 130–3
work spaces 62–5, 131
World Design and Trade headquarters 132

Y
Yoo Apartments 68, 92, 93

Our thanks are due to the many people who helped in the creation of this book:

To our colleagues on the Interior Architecture programmes at Middlesex University – in particular Jon Mortimer, Tony Side, Tony Smart and Paul Tomkinson – for their encouragement and for holding the fort on those occasions when the book had to take precedence over everything else. To the practices and individuals who contributed images and assistance: Frans Burrows and David Bishop at Bluebottle; Tim Mutton and Lucy Porter at Blacksheep; Nick Coombe; Jonathan Stickland; Nick Pettersen at Universal Design Studio; Carlos Virgile, Phoebe Chung, Katy Bottomley and Anne Hoyer at Virgile and Stone; Arwen Nicholson. Thanks also to Lynne Mesher, Graeme Brooker, Patrick Hannay and Ro Spankie, and finally, but not least, to Hazel House for proofreading when we had become book-blind and to Brian Morris, Caroline Walmsley, Leafy Robinson and Natalia Price-Cabrera at AVA Publishing, without whom this book would not exist.

credits

p.4, Chapter 0: Photograph by Jannes Linders, provided courtesy of Virgile and Stone; Chapter 1: Photograph by James Morris <www.jamesmorris.info>, provided courtesy of Jonathan Stickland, Chapter 2: Photograph by James Morris <www.jamesmorris.info>, provided courtesy of Nick Coombe / p.5, Chapter 3: Photograph provided courtesy of Nick Coombe; Chapter 4: Photograph by Francesca Yorke, provided courtesy of Blacksheep; Chapter 5: Photograph provided courtesy of Blacksheep; Chapter 6: Photograph provided courtesy of Blacksheep / p.13: Graves, M. 1982. Interview with Hiroshi Watanabe. *Architecture & Urbanism*. No.147 (December 1982) / p.14: Photograph by James Morris <www.jamesmorris.info>, provided courtesy of Jonathan Stickland / p.21: Blake, P. 1977. *Form Follows Fiasco: Why Modern Architecture Hasn't Worked*. Boston/Toronto: Little, Brown / p.36: Helmut Jahn. Murphy/Jahn [online]. [Accessed 12 June 2007]. Published on the World Wide Web: <http://www.murphyjahn.com> / p.38: Johnson, P. 1979. *Philip Johnson: Writings*. New York: Oxford University Press / p.41: Taniguchi, Y. 2004. Interview with Jeffrey Brown on 29 November 2004. New York [online]. [Accessed 12 June 2007]. Published on the World Wide Web: <www.pbs.org/newshour> / p.44: Photograph by James Morris <www.jamesmorris.info>, provided courtesy of Nick Coombe / p.62: Karan, D. Quoteopia. 2005. [online]. [Accessed 12 June 2007]. Published on the World Wide Web: <http://www.quoteopia.com> / p.64: Philippe Starck, quoted in Cooper, E., Doze, P. Leville, E. (eds). 2003. *Starck by Starck*. Cologne: Taschen / p.66: Le Corbusier, C. E. J. Thinkexist.com. Date unknown. [online]. [Accessed 9 July 2007]. Published on the World Wide Web: <http://www.thinkexist.com> / p.76: Photograph provided courtesy of Nick Coombe / p.109: Photographs, left to right, by P. Uzunova, P. Uzunova, Boris Katsman, Sybille Yates / p.110: Photographs, left to right, by Victor Burnside, Paul Paladin, Selahattin Bayram, Joan Gomez Pons / p.111: Photographs, left to right, by RAFA? FABRYKIEWICZ, Cecilia Lim H M, P. Uzunova, Tyler Boyes / p.112: Photographs, left to right, by vnlit, Kurt Tutschek, Perov Stanislav, Otmar Smit / p.113: Photographs, left to right, by Kerry Garvey, Marco Regalia, Ramzi Hachicho, Jan Matoska / p.114: Photographs, left to right, by Robert Kyllo, James Robey, Nemanja Glumac, Tyler Olson / p.115: Photographs, left to right, by Anita, cloki, Victoria Alexandrova, unknown / p.118: Photograph by Francesca Yorke, provided courtesy of Blacksheep / p.121: Piano, R. 2006 Interview with Liz Martin on 16 January 2006. Atlanta [online]. [Accessed 12 June 2007]. Published on the World Wide Web: <http://archinect.com> / p.146: Photograph provided courtesy of Blacksheep